Vijayanagara

A Forgotten Empire of Poetesses

Part I. The Voice of Gaṅgādevī

Lidia Sudyka

Kraków 2013

Reviewed by:
Prof. Chettiarthodi Rajendran
Dr. Cezary Galewicz

Technical editor:
Marek Sudyka

Cover design:
Emilia Dajnowicz
Cover photo:
Pārvatī and maids (Lepakshi Temple) by Lidia Sudyka

Proofreading:
Ramon Shindler

The book was published thanks to the financial support of Faculty of Philology, Jagiellonian University.

ISBN 978-83-7638-379-8

Published in the e-book form plus paper copies.
The primary version of the book is the paper format.

Księgarnia Akademicka sp. z o.o.
31-008 Kraków, ul. św. Anny 6
e-mail: akademicka@akademicka.pl
www.akademicka.pl

Contents

Acknowledgements

I began reading the first excerpts of the *Madhurāvijaya*—or the "Conquest of Madhurā", authored by Gaṅgādevī in 2007—first out of curiosity and then with growing interest. I obtained those fragments of the poem from my colleague Cezary Galewicz, Ph.D., who at that time was working on his book "A Commentator in Service of the Empire. Sāyaṇa and the Royal Project of Commenting on the whole of the Veda". It was not easy for me to find an edition of the whole of Gaṅgā's work. Finally, I managed to obtain not only this text, but also a *campū* (a poem in verse and prose) *Varadāmbikāpariṇaya*, or the "Marriage of Varadāmbikā", authored by another Vijayanagara poetess, Tirumalāmbā. Those acquisitions made me think about the position of women literati at the Vijayanagara courts. Who were they? And what kind of lives did they live? Would it be possible to regain some scraps of the Vijayanagara past thanks to their writings, even if there were ideology hidden behind certain statements and constructs? Such eulogies written by poets usually betray the intentions of their patrons.

Knowing Sanskrit classical literary tradition, i.e. *kāvya*,[1] as highly conventionalised, mainly concentrated on playing with language and conventional images, it would be difficult to expect Sanskrit poems composed by women to allow us to sketch an 'alternative' tradition of women's writing, in a way different from

[1] More about characteristic features of *kāvya* in: Lienhard 1984.

the dominant male tradition. It can be hoped, however, that a distinctive female voice could be heard at least in passages devoted to certain themes connected strongly with female life, such as childbirth and pregnancy.

I started reading the works of the two poetesses with these questions and observations in mind.

In 2009, from 15th July to 30th August, I had a chance to use the resources of the Kern Institute Library in Leiden thanks to the Gonda Foundation Fellowship in the International Institute of Asian Studies. At that time I was able to write some parts of the present book; however, in the next two years, for different reasons, I could hardly continue my work. It was possible to 're-new the acquaintance' with both Sanskrit women writers in the academic year 2012/2013 during my sabbatical leave granted by the Faculty of Philology at the Jagiellonian University in Cracow, Poland. I would like to thank them for this chance that first enabled me to commence the work and then finish it.

I have also collected some more debts of gratitude which I would like to acknowledge here.

I am indebted to Dr. Herman Tieken for his help and interest in my indological quest.

I am also grateful to Professors Rajendran Chettiarthodi and Cezary Galewicz who kindly agreed to review the present volume for the publisher.

I also thank all the authors of not yet published articles who shared with me the outcome of their latest research. These are Prof. Yaroslav Vassilkov, Prof. Yigal Bronner, Dr. Anna Trynkowska, Lidia Szczepanik, M.A. and Tomasz Winiarski, M.A.

My thanks are due to Dr. Anna Nitecka for allowing me to publish some of her photos taken during her trips to Tamil Nadu and my colleague and friend Prof. Marzenna Czerniak-Drożdżowicz for her support.

Many thanks, to Ms. Maria Skakuj-Puri and Ms. Katarzyna Pażucha, who helped me obtain numerous books and articles.

At the last stage of my work, Ms. Lidia Szczepanik, a Ph.D. candidate at the Institute of Oriental Studies, Jagiellonian University, presented me with a newly published selection of stanzas from the *Madhurāvijaya* with a translation by Shankar Rajaraman and Venetia Kotamraju. The nicely translated verses brought new energy to finish my own book.

I also owe a deep debt of gratitude to Ms. Agata Lenard for her careful reading and editing of my draft as well as Mr. Ramon Shindler from the Institute of English Studies (Jagiellonian University) for proofreading.

Many other friends and my family stood by me in many ways, silently and patiently tolerating my full-time preoccupation with the Vijayanagara poetesses. Both of them, Gaṅgādevī and Tirumalāmbā, wrote for their men; following their example, I would like to dedicate my book to my husband, Marek, for supporting me all the time.

Lidia Sudyka
June 2013

Introduction

Bilhaṇa, *Vikramāṅkadevacarita* 1.26[2]

pṛthvīpateḥ santi na yasya pārśve
kavīśvarās tasya kuto yaśāṃsi /
bhūpāḥ kiyanto na babhūvur urvyāṃ
jānāti nāmāpi na ko'pi teṣām //

Where could the lord of the earth have fame from
if there were no lords of poetry at his side?
How many kings lived on the earth
whose names are not even known to anybody?[3]

The history of Indian southern kingdoms, although greatly advanced in the 20th century, still needs a lot of consideration. One of the sources which should be seriously examined, while reconstructing the history of the South of India, is that of epic poems, i.e. *mahākāvyas* or *sargabandhas* (epic poems in verse) and *campūs* (verse and prose works),[4] written at the courts of local sovereigns. The vast treasury of *mahākāvyas* and *campūs* which

---

[2] Bühler 1875: 3.

[3] All the translations from Sanskrit are mine unless otherwise stated.

[4] Also *sandeśakāvyas* ('messenger' poems) should be examined thoroughly although these works were quite often created by authors not connected with courts. Nevertheless, they contain a surprising amount of information concerning history, society and religion in South India. Unfortunately, little research on South Indian *sandeśakāvyas* has been done so far although the situation has been changing recently—new translations have appeared (e.g. *The Mission of the Goose* of Vedānta Deśika, transl. by Yigal Bronner and David Shulman,

were written in the South after the 10th century A.D. has a lot to offer. The author of the monograph "A Historical Survey of Sanskrit *Mahākāvyas*", L. Sulochana Devi, mentions 41 Sanskrit *mahākāvyas* produced only in Kerala after the 11th century. The "Studies in Campū Literature" by C. R. Deshpande contains a register of 390 Sanskrit *campūs*, most of which originated in medieval South India. Some of these *mahākāvyas* and *campūs* were published in the South of India in the 20th century and yet failed to attract the attention of Western scholarship. Only a few of them have been translated and annotated by Indian scholars. The monographs on these works are almost non-existent. Among the Indian Sanskritists who have brought to light many interesting Sanskrit *mahākāvyas* that originated in the South of India, at the very least the name of V. Raghavan should be mentioned here. Of course, as with any Sanskrit work composed within the *kāvya* tradition, the literary works first of all fulfil the conventional requirements specific to their genres, yet, nevertheless, they contain valuable information indispensable for writing the political, social and cultural history of the South of India. The medieval *mahākāvyas*, i.e. 'great/major poems' in verse (*sargabandha*[5]), prose (*gadya*) or mixture of verse and prose (*campū*), represent court culture and their authors were patronised by the kings and local rulers. If so, it is reasonable to presume that the examples of these genres, except for their aesthetic aims described by numerous Indian theoreticians of literature, could also fulfil special tasks serving the needs of their patrons. It is not difficult to accept such an opinion in the case of the so-called historical *mahākāvyas*. These Sanskrit poems are in fact pieces of panegyric literature.

Clay Sanskrit Library, 2009), interesting articles have been written (by Steven Hopkins, Yigal Bronner, Lidia Szczepanik) and in August 2013, at the Hebrew University of Jerusalem, an international group of scholars will be working on the project "Mapping the World through Courier Poems".

[5] The term *mahākāvya* in its narrower sense refers to *sargabandha*—an epic poem in verse consisting of several chapters known as *sargas*.

The rulers and their ancestors are eulogised in them. However, a great number of the *mahākāvyas* are based on the *Mahābhārata* or *Rāmāyaṇa*. One may wonder whether also in this case the work in question can provide any extratextual pieces of information. It turns out that when analysed in the broad historical context from which they arose, they also reveal their crucial involvement in articulating the polities of medieval India.[6]

The present book is a part of a bigger project focusing on glimpses of history of the Vijayanagara Empire hidden under the poetic matter authored by women. Part I concentrates on the *sargabandha Madhurāvijaya* composed by Gaṅgādevī and the forthcoming Part II deals with *Varadāmbikāpariṇaya Campū* by Tirumalāmbā. The aim of a so-called historical *mahākāvya* or *campū* was to describe the victories and successes of its hero. The hero is always presented as abounding in all the qualities of a powerful ruler, no matter what the historical truth was. As C. R. Deshpande notes, and his remark can be extended to the *mahākāvya*, that it was conventional for the *campū* genre to "make use of such already current ideas as the fame of the king in question wandering in all three worlds making them white, his enemies turning pale at the mention of his name, the enemies' wives leading a miserable life in forests, etc." (Deshpande 1992: 188).[7] However, behind the conventional *kāvya* images, there might be a historically important message which should not be overlooked. And in this case the king's fame is really a crucial issue. The eulogies,

[6] The best example can be provided by the *Kirātārjunīya* of Bhāravi; see for instance: Viswanathan Peterson 2003; Sudyka 2011.

[7] The manner of describing the king and all his deeds, even his everyday routine, by means of images of all that could possibly be shining and white in colour, the colour which according to convention should be associated with fame, was omnipresent in Southern Indian literature. An interesting study entitled "Royal Eulogy as World History. Rethinking Copper-plate Inscriptions in Cōḻa India" with its subchapter "Gathering and Emitting Light" authored by Daud Ali addresses this subject (Ali 2000: 203–205).

be it inscriptional or "textual", were made in order to proliferate the king's fame across his kingdom and beyond its boundaries for the king's contemporaries as well as for future generations. However, links with the past were also extremely important. That is the reason for a long list of predecessors to be so often given in eulogies and mythical connections with the remote past to be presented in them as well. The task of the poet was to link aptly his royal patron with the past, show the glorious present and in this way open possibilities for "everlasting fame". These Sanskrit *kāvya* works presented royal histories and they must have aspired to enter the domain of the public political texts articulating the kingly power. Besides, each author was a witness to the times in which he or she wrote. In that way the authors and their outlooks are part and parcel of history. As Yigal Bronner aptly shows in his articles, Sanskrit authors, at least some of them, despite the possible limitations created by poetical convention, were able to show their own worldviews and attitudes.[8]

A great number of books and articles have been written on *kāvya* conventions, stereotyped heroes and heroines as well as genre requirements and stylistic features. Now is the time to look beyond conventions in order to find scattered pieces of information which could be useful in the reconstruction of the forgotten past. It is hoped that the present study will bring to light some data concerning the Vijayanagara Empire culture and past but most importantly show the court poets and their patrons reflected in poems. However, as we are dealing with women's writing here, it is expected that it would be possible to recognize Vijayanagara royal women's views and feelings and perhaps understand what their position was, in the literary marketplace included. The presumption is that the experience of women shaped by their gender could have an impact on their writings. Nevertheless, the question arises whether it will be true in the case of highly conventionalised Sanskrit poems.

---

[8] Bronner (forthcoming); Bronner 2010.

It is a demanding task to analyse women authors' cultural contribution both in Sanskrit and vernaculars. First of all, not many literary works authored by women have survived to this day. There are poetesses whose writings are lost, whereas some other compositions, mainly in vernaculars, have never been committed to writing. On the other hand, not all preserved manuscripts may have been brought to light and published. Again those which are published may be understudied or have never been studied at all. The printed texts usually contain introductions limited to very basic facts only.

It is not the case of the *Madhurāvijaya* or "The Conquest of Madhurā", however. The text was found purely by chance in 1916 in a private library in Trivandrum, as a part of a collection of Sanskrit works, then published by Pandit V. Srinivasa Sastri of the Travancore Archaeological Department (Aiyangar Krishnaswamy 2003: 28). Two more manuscripts of the *Madhurāvijaya* were discovered, neither of them complete or in a better condition than the one found first. The fourth existing manuscript is in the Punjab University Library in Lahore. In 1924 the second edition of the *Madhurāvijaya* appeared (ed. G. Harihara Sastri & V. Srinivasa Sastri, Trivandrum: The Sridhara Power Press). The next edition cum English translation was published in 1957 by S. Thiruvenkatachari.[9] It is provided with a lengthy historical *Introduction* by the editor and translator. Then, in 1969 Subrahmaṇyaśāstrī prepared another edition, trying to fill some lacunae of the manuscripts and offering Sanskrit commentary as well as introductory essays. This edition, to my knowledge, is absent from European libraries. In 1989 Kuśālappa Gauḍa edited the text and translated it into Kannada. In 2001 Sharada Mishra produced another editition and translation of the text into Hindi.

[9] I am following the Trivandrum edition of 1924 and Thiruvenkatachari's edition of the *Madhurāvijayam*. I had at my disposal only some excerpts copied from Subrahmaṇyaśāstrī's edtion, which I could consult. As to the translations, in several cases I am indebted to Thiruvenkatachari's ones; however, because of different reasons, I do not quote them in my book.

There are two monographs on this *mahākāvya* published recently. In 2007 Sharada Mishra published her study under the title *Rājarānī Gaṅgādevī aur unkā kāvyaśilp* (queen Gaṅgādevī and her Poetic Craftsmanship). She is mainly concerned with poetic figures and other stylistic devices of the epic poem, although the first chapter deals in short with its historical aspect referring to S. Thiruvenkatachari, Venkataramanayya and other sources published decades ago. Mishra also discusses structural parallels to the works of famous Sanskrit poets. B. A. Dodamani's *Gaṅgādevī's Madhurāvijayam. A literary Study* edited one year later accordingly to the book's title is dedicated to the stylistic level of the poem. It seems that both books do not take into account new findings and hypothesis concerning Vijayanagara history.

Longer or shorter excerpts from the *Madhurāvijayam* Sanskrit text, sometimes together with their translations or translations alone, appeared in different books, e.g. "Sources of Vijayanagara History" (Aiyangar Krishnaswamy 2003) and "Kingship: state and religion in South India according to South Indian historical biographies of kings (*Madhurāvijaya, Acyutarāyābhudaya* and *Vemabbhūpalacarita*)", an unpublished Ph.D. dissertation of D. Sridhara Babu, Georg-August-Universität zu Göttingen.

In 2013 a translation of two hundred selected verses from the *Madhurāvijaya* into English, together with the Sanskrit text of the translated stanzas, was published as a jointly effort of Venetia Kotamraju and Shankar Rajaraman.[10]

All the editors did not have an access to the Lahore manuscript, which although incomplete and consisting of seven *sargas* only, could provide some missing fragments from earlier cantos. The

[10] Kotamraju and Rajaraman on the website `www.rasalabooks.com` mention also two recent monographs on the Madhurāvijaya to which I had no access: Kannan, K. S. 2010. *Madhurāvijayam of Gangādevī: A historical work of* 14th *Century in Sanskrit (cantos 8 and 9)*. Bangalore University, Bangalore; Krishnamachariar, A. 2010. *Gangādevī's Madhurāvijayam*. Shriranganachiar Publishers, Srirangam.

task of a critical edition of the *Madhurāvijaya* undertaken in the 20th century is still awaiting its completion. Nevertheless, it should be stated that just since the moment of its discovery after six centuries of oblivion, the work of Gaṅgādevī has attracted the attention of historians as well as that of literary critics. In fact, the *Madhurāvijaya*, this fourteenth-century *mahākāvya* written by Gaṅgādevī, who introduces herself as a beloved of Kampana, the son of Bukka I of the Sangama Dynasty, is viewed differently by scholars nowadays. Velcheru Narayana Rao, David Shulman and Sanjay Subrahmanyam call it "the literary celebration of Kampana's conquest" (Rao, Shulman & Subrahmanyam 1992: 29) and seem to treat it mainly as a literary work devoid of significance as a historical document. Some other refer to it as a source of reliable historical information. Perhaps the truth is somewhere in between. Definitely, Gaṅgādevī's composition fulfils the requirements prescribed for its literary genre thoroughly. However, the poetess speaks not about the mythical or remote past but about the events she witnessed herself. That is why we cannot fail to take into account her voice while reconstructing the early history of the Vijayanagara Empire, which still poses questions difficult to answer decisively. We shall consult other literary works mentioning personages and facts with which she presents us. Inscriptions from that period will be also taken into account. The degree of historicity of the work and other problems possible to address definitely stimulate interest in the *Madhurāvijaya* and could make further investigations rewarding.

Tirumalāmbā, on the other hand, associated with the court of Acyutarāya (Tuluva Dynasty), and her literary works, occasionally mentioned shortly in different articles and monographs, do not seem to draw similar scholars' attention. Fortunately, there is an edition of her *campū*, entitled *Varadāmbikāpariṇaya*, published together with an English translation and a 29-page-long Introduction by its editor and translator Suryakanta. There are also some Sanskrit verses eulogising her kingly "employer" and then husband, Acyutarāya (reigned: 1529–1542) of the Vijayanagara Tuluva dynasty. They are preserved in temple inscriptions in different places, such as Hampi, Kalahasti, Lepakshi and Srirangam (Skr. Śrīraṅgam). There are also mentions about other works of this royal poetess which have not been preserved. It seems that she was a really prolific writer.

What life did the two poetesses belonging to different centuries and courts of different dynasty rulers live? Would it be possible to collect some scraps of it from among the verses celebrating their kings?

Chapter 1 Vijayanagara Women—Whisperings of Inscripions[11]

Before we embark on any closer inspection of both texts, it would be worth thinking about the position of women in medieval South India and their career opportunities, especially in the field of literature

According to the Portuguese traveller, chronicler and horse trader, Fernão Nunes (also known as Fernao Nuniz), who spent three years (1535–1537) in Vijayanagara, there were women at the king's court responsible for writing down all the accounts and expenses, while the task of some others was to note down all the happenings in the kingdom and compare their books with those of outside writers (Sewell 1992: 248–249, 382). There were also women who held offices of responsibility in the state (Sewell 1992: 383). Mahalingam, in his study *Administration and Social Life under Vijayanagar. Part II. Social Life*, says that:

> (...) from the evidence of Nuniz one may assume that women were employed for the management of the zenana. It is highly doubtful if

[11] I allude to Noboru Karashima's declaration: "I always start my study by reading inscriptions, as many of them as possible, so that I may listen to their 'whisperings'."(Karashima 2001: 56).

> women were appointed to offices of responsibility in the government. (Mahalingam 1975: 42)

In fact, we know very little about women's lives and status in the period of the Sangama dynasty. *Kāvya* usually shows them in connection with the erotic emotion (*śṛṅgārarasa*) and literature created at that time did the same, which makes the picture lacking perhaps not so in colours as in details. There is one more source which can yield glimpses into women's lives, namely inscriptions. Perhaps it is worth quoting Cynthia Talbot, who investigated the position of women in Kākatīya Andhra:

> The roles that women could assume in medieval society were not solely domestic, as one might believe from reading the *dharmaśāstra* texts. The temple institution was the primary public arena for women in Kakatiya Andhra. There they could hold honored positions as officials in charge of treasury (EI 6.15; SII 6.89 and 228), as well as serving as temple dancers (SII 4.700, SII 5.140). In several temples in coastal Andhra, endowments were administered by the collective body of temple women known as the Sani 300 (e.g., SII 5.161). Most of these temple women, or *guḍisāni*, were daughters of respectable men like *nāyakas* or *seṭṭis*. (...) Political authority could also be publicly wielded by aristocratic women. (Talbot 2001: 84)

One can expect that the situation in the same territory and neighbouring ones under the rule of Vijayanagara, i.e. several decades later, would not be exposed to drastic changes.

The corpus of Karnataka texts written during the rule of the Sangama dynasty between 1336 to 1485[12] is not very rich in records mentioning women, nevertheless, it cannot be neglected as a source of information. We learn from the slab inscription in the Someśvara temple that during the rule of Devarāya I, when Śaṃkaradēva was his *mahāpradhāna* (chief minister) governing Bārakūra-rājya, one Jogi-seṭṭi with his wife Rāmakka and their

[12] Gopal & Ritti 2004.

son Cikki-Seṭṭi made a grant for a regular supply of rice to feed a *brāhmaṇa* on the occasion of *rudrapūjā* in the temple of Sōmanāthadēva of Mūrukeri (Gopal & Ritti 2004: 1052–1053). It is a collective, family donation. However, studying inscriptions proves that individual donations by women happened quite regularly. It also turns out that women could be land owners. According to Indian legal literature, women's personal property *(strīdhana)* was restricted to jewellery and some other movable goods. In the inscriptional corpus one comes across a text dated 1366 which informs us that during the reign of Bukka I, Viṭhapa-daṃḍanāyaka had purchased land from one Sōvaladēvi[13] and granted the income from the land for the offerings, a perpetual lamp and for feeding the *brāhmaṇas* in the temple of Śrīkṛṣṇa at Udupi (Gopal & Ritti 2004: 151–152). The inscription from Kāḍūru (Udupi District) dated 1371 records that a lady Dugu-binnāṇitti, after the death of her son, arranged for the regular feeding of one *brāhmaṇa* by granting a piece of land which she purchased for that purpose (Gopal & Ritti 2004: 215–216). Padumaladēvi, a daughter of Kāmadēva, a scion of the royal Kadamba family, arranged for feeding 12 *brāhmaṇas*, including hiring a cook, in the shelter (*chatra*) attached to the temple of Omaṃjūru. For this purpose she purchased land, as the inscription from Banavāsi dated 1387 records (Gopal & Ritti 2004: 478–501). Another woman, Nāgavve, the wife of Rāmaṇṇa-seṭṭi, made a grant of money to the temple of Somanāthadeva of Maṇigārakēri for everyday worship of Śiva in his Rudra form (*rudra-pūjā*) and feeding three *brāhmaṇas* as well as providing different types of lamps and *pañcāmṛta*[14] on every full moon day (*pūrṇimā*) (Gopal & Ritti 2004: 333–334). The inscription from Āraga (Shivamogga District), dated 1376, records the construction of a hall for religious gatherings

[13] The transliteration of names according to Gopal and Ritti. Later on I use the Sanskritised version of some of these names.

[14] The mixture of five nectars, usually milk, yoghurt, ghee, honey and sugar.

(*sabhā-maṇḍapa*) in the temple of Vīrabhadra by Maṇjādēvi, wife of Vēdagiri Virupaṇṇa (Gopal & Ritti 2004: 315–316). The inscription from Tirumani, Kolar Disctrict, dated 1397, marks important irrigation works ordered by Jommādēvi, a daughter of Virūpādēvi, who was again a daughter of Bukka I. Jommādēvi's minister, Nāgarāja, made a contract for digging a channel to fill a tank.[15]

These inscriptions, although low in number, prove that women, regardless of their social status, could buy and sell land as well as donate it individually to the temple. One of the above mentioned women was the wife of Rāmaṇṇa-seṭṭi, and *seṭṭi* forms a caste name of members of merchant communities in South India. Another belonged to the ancient royal Karnataka family of Kadambas. They could also donate money, sacrificial utensils or found temple buildings. The inscription from Tirumaṇi shows that women from the Sangama family financed irrigation of the area.

Among the material gathered by Gopal and Ritti, there is a number of inscriptions commemorating deaths of women. Some of them committed *satī*.[16] Another group of inscriptions, which is less numerous, records the death by *sanyasana-vidhi*. It turns out that these women were disciples of Jaina teachers or ascetics. The inscription from Hire Āvali (Shivamogga District), dated 1396, informs that Kāmi-gauṇḍi, wife of Kāna-Rāmaṇa, daughter-in-law of Bommara and Beca-gauṇḍa, the chief of Jiḍḍaḷige and Āvalipura, died by the rite (*vidhi*) of *sanyasana* (abstinence from all kinds of food). She was a disciple of Siddhānti-yatīśa (Gopal & Ritti 2004: 579–580). Tavananadi inscription, dated 1372, registers the death

[15] EC X.10; EI: 232, 285.

[16] For instance certain Nāgamma, after her husband died an unnatural death, receiving assurance from her father-in-law that he would set up a hero-stone for her husband, committed *satī* (Inscription form Nādūru, 1377 A.D.); the inscription on a *sati*-stone from Kaṇavi, Gadag District, dated 1407 A.D., informs us that Nāgāyi and Dēmāyi died along with their husband (Gopal & Ritti 2004: 175–176, 812–813).

by *samādhi-vidhi* of Bommakka, daughter of Viṭṭhala and wife of Bomma-gauḍa. She was a disciple of Simhanandi of Balātkāra-gaṇa (Gopal & Ritti 2004: 226–227). Another woman, Bommi-gauṇḍi, wife of Beci-gauṇḍa from Āvali and a disciple of Jina-pati M(R?)āmaracandra-maladhāridēva, also died by *sanyasana-samādhi-vidhi*. There is an interesting statement that describes her meditation on Jina being so deep that even in speech and thought she did not remember her sons and grandsons (*Jinara nenevutta vacanadoḷ manasinoḷaṃ putrapautraṃ toravuttaṃ yenagīga paṃcapadagaḷe ghanavenutale muḍihi svarggamaṃ neṟe paḍedaḷu*—Gopal & Ritti 2004: 750). This is the evidence that not only Jaina asetics, teachers, kings and other male members of Jain community practiced the rituals through which death was invited.[17]

The way of renunciation was also open for the lay womenfolk—members of families. The case that women were disciples of male ascetics and monks has been already proved by the above-quoted Sangama inscriptions. On the other hand, as Aloka Parasher-Sen states in her article "Renunciation in the Jain Tradition", women "were allowed to become nuns, and as senior nuns, had monks as disciples".[18]

Inscriptions from the Tuluva dynasty period depicting women-donors are more frequent. The inscriptions registered during the twelve years of Acyutarāya's reign only in two temples—Veṅkaṭeśvara Temple at Tirumalai and Govindarāja Temple in Tirupati—belong to two types of donors: the Queen (4 records) and as V. Vijayaraghavacharya, the editor and the translator of these inscriptions calls them, the temple damsels (12 records) (Vijayaraghavacharya 1984: VII). As that Queen is Varadāmbikā, the heroine of our *campū*, the records will be referred to in the

[17] Read more about *samādhi*, *ārādhanā* and *sanyasana-vidhi* in: *Inviting Death: Indian attitude towards the ritual death* (Settar 1989).

[18] Parasher-Sen 2001: 471.

forthcoming Part II and its chapters devoted to the poem. The same concerns the poetess Tirumalāmbā, whose name appears in inscriptions quite often. Among the temple women we can find one Govindasāni, who on 8th July 1530 donated money

> (...) for the purpose of providing for Śrī Gōvindarājan an offering of 1 atirasa-paḍi on the day of Māśi, 1 atirasa-paḍi on the day of Paṅguni-Uttiram, (...) and 1 atirasa-paḍi on the day of Pāḍiya-vēṭṭai (hunting festival), altogether 6 atirasa-paḍi in each year while seated in your maṇṭapam constructed by you on the bank of the Gōvindapushkariṇī (...).
> (Vijayaraghavacharya 1984: 14)

The sum of 300 *paṇam* was meant for "the improvement and excavation of the irrigation tanks and channels in the temple villages" (Vijayaraghavacharya 1984: 14). There were also records concerning temple dancers. One of them is in favour of Muddukuppāyi:

> (...) as you are orderd to serve as the dancer in the temple of Śrī Vēṅkaṭēśa at Tirumalai by Achyutarāya Mahārāya, you are entitled to receive one taḷigai-prasādam daily for your maintenance from this day onwards from the temple of Śrī Gōvindarāja abiding in Tirupati. In this manner you are authorised to serve through the succession of your descendants in the temple of Śrī Vēṅkaṭēśa and to receive one taḷigai-prasādam as long as the moon and the sun shine.
> (Vijayaraghavacharya 1984: 24)

Here the dancer sent by the king was provided with food gift or *prasādam*. Temple dancers were also donors to the temple and in such a case they were entitled to have their share in food offerings, as was recorded on 13th July 1535 for Liṅgi and Tiruvēṅkaṭamāṇikkam, daughters of Tippasāni, one of the Emperumānaḍiyaḷ (temple damsels):

> You are entitled to receive the quarter share of the offered appam and dōsai prasādam due to the donor. The balance of the prasādam

> we shall set apart for distribution at the early sandhi.
> (Vijayaraghavacharya 1984: 97)

Some inscriptions registered in Bhatkal area bring the name of "the Mahāmaṇḍalēśvara Chennadevi Ammanavaru daughter-in-law of Devarasa-vodeya as ruling Bhatkala and other *Rājyas* from her capital Sangītapura" (Raghavendra 1941: 38). According to Noboru Karashima, the formal title of *mahāmaṇḍalēśvara* refers to administrators (Karashima 1985: 24) or governors of the provinces. Sangītapura, at present the village Haduvalli of Bhatkal Taluk in North Kanara District of Karnataka State, was a well-known cultural centre of Jaina culture. Chennadevi was not the only queen ruling in this region and her inscriptions show the strong position of women there. In the inscription from 23rd October 1542 it is stated that she

> (...) granted to Naranadeva-Nayaka sister's son of his officer named Linga-Nayaka, a land having the sowing capacity of ten and a half *mudis* of paddy, belonging to the palace, after detenanted it from the previous tenants (...). It is stated that the land should pass to the female descendants as gift (*peṇṇige dāna*) or to the male descendants by right of succession (*gaṇḍige mūla*).
> (Raghavendra 1941: 38)

It is worth mentioning the in this region as well as in Tulu country and Kerala the matrilineal system of inheritance was practised by various communities (*aliyasantana*—i.e. a sister's son was the successor).

Summing up, according to epigraphical evidence, women in the Vijayanagara period could be individual donors, they owned land and could transfer land rights to others, and it seems that they could hold honoured positions in the temples. Definitely, educated women, as attested by European travellers, held important positions at royal courts. Perhaps their importance was hidden behind the walls of the zenana enclosure but not necessarily restricted to it. On the other hand, a dancer can be sent to the temple as a kind of gift. The examples of women-rulers in the Vijayanagara period can be provided, too.

Let us now try to amplify the whispering of inscriptions applying to Vijayanagara women's writing.

Chapter 2
The Woman-writer Gaṅgādevī Speaks

2.1. Gaṅgādevī introduces herself

Rajaśekhara, *Kāvyamīmāṃsā*[19]

puruṣavat yoṣito 'pi kavībhaveyuḥ / saṃskāro hy ātmani samavaiti, na straiṇaṃ pauruṣaṃ vā vibhāgam apekṣate / śrūyante dṛśyante ca rājaputryo mahāmātyaduhitaro gaṇikāḥ kautukibhāryāś ca śāstra-prahatabuddhayaḥ kavayaś ca /

Women can be poets as men are. Mental impressions assemble in the soul, it does not require discrimination between men and women. One can hear about or see princesses, daughters of ministers, courtesans and wives of artists having mind trained in scholarly disciplines and composing poetry.

Some scholars expressed their doubts about female authorship of such poems as the *Madhurāvijayam* and suggested the possibility that these were court poets or the gurus of the queens who wrote the compositions and ascribed them to these female authors.[20]

---

[19] Rājaśekhara 2000: 116.

[20] e.g.: "The lady poet (or may we perhaps think rather of her pandit teacher?) was an accomplished Sanskrit scholar (...)" (Emeneau 1985: 401).

If we consider the possibility that those queens, or at least some of them, were in fact courtesans 'wedded' to a king, the chances for their literary education cannot be questioned. As A. K. Ramanujan, Velcheru Narayana Rao and David Shulman write:

> (...) the courtesan enjoyed a freedom usually reserved for men; not only did she not suffer from many restrictions imposed on women but she was given the same honor shown to poets in a royal court. Names of great courtesans such as Mācaladevi are known in literature dating from the Kākatīya period. Some, such as the learned Raṅgājamma, were prominent poets in the Nāyaka courts. (Ramanujan, Rao & Shulman 1994: 27)

No one questions the role in the literary marketplace of the courtesan, Madhuravāṇī, who lived at the court of Raghunāthanāyaka. Some information about her relationship with King Raghunātha can be acquired through her elaborated work *Śrīrāmāyaṇasārakāvyatilakam.*

The *Krīḍābhirāmamu*, a parodic work of a Telugu poet Vinukōṇḍa Vallabharāya living in the first half of the fifteenth century, introduces a courtesan favoured by the great king Pratāparudra in such words:

> She is famous all over the world
> as the great preceptor of love as laid down
> in the Vedic Science of desire. She won the highest respect
> of the assembly of scholars, presided over
> by the King himself, Pratāpa-rudra. Don't you recognize
> this Mācaladevi, the well-known whore? (180)
> (Rao & Shulman transl. 2002: 8)

Judging by the contents of the *Madhurāvijayam*, Gaṅgādevī definitely was not one of the royal queens with a higher status. The kings and princes had many wives, as we know, but among them only a few principal ones whose sons could inherit the kingdom (Mahalingam 1975: 39–40). Nowhere in the poem is there even the slightest hint that Gaṅgādevī was important in the hierarchy of the royal ladies.

In stanza 17, *sarga* 3, we come across information that King Bukka I arranged for marriages of his son:

athainam āsāditayauvanodayaṃ
narendrakanyābhir ayojayan nṛpaḥ /
ghanāgamaḥ saṃbhṛtaratnasaṃpadaṃ
varāpagābhir nidhim ambhasām iva // MV 3.17 //[21]

Then the King joined him,
who attained bloom of his youth,
with the royal daughters,
like the advent of rainy season unites the ocean,
receptacle of accumulated jewels,
with the most excellent rivers.

Definitely these were political marriages. As Daud Ali points out:

> Relations of friendship, fealty and even favour could be established through the 'gift of a virgin' (*kanyādāna*). In some cases, the gift of a king's daughter to an overlord's household was expected as a sign of loyalty (...).
> (Ali 2004: 51)

The next stanza of the *Madhurāvijayam* promises the name of Kampana's chief consort, however all what is left contains several comparisons:

śacīva śakrasya rameva śārṅgiṇaḥ satīva śambho
Like Śacī to Śakra (Indra), like Ramā (Lakṣmī) to Śārṅgin (Visṇu), like Satī (Pārvatī) to Śambhu (Śiva)...

Perhaps the name of the principal consort, or most probably consorts as the previous sentence mentions kings' daughters (three of them or more?) compared respectively to Śacī, Lakṣmī and Pārvatī, came at that moment. Unfortunately this part of the

[21] The Sanskrit text of the *Madhurāvijayam* is given after consulting the editions of 1924 and 1957. In several cases I introduced my own emendations.

manuscript is missing. Was the name of Gaṅgādevī mentioned in this stanza? There are certain grounds to doubt it. If she was a princess, there would be a chance to add such an important piece of information about her parentage in some other passages of her work.

Yet another passage, namely 7.39–41, put before the readers' eyes the pair: Kampana and Gaṅgā:

atha kampanṛpo 'pi kṛtyavit
kṛtasandhyāsamayocitakriyaḥ /
avadat savidhe sthitāṃ priyāṃ
bhuvi gaṅgetyabhinanditāhvayām // MV 7.39 //

Then the conscientious King Kampana,
after performing worship proper for the twilight,
addressed his beloved who was near him
and who was greeted with the name Gaṅgā in this world.

kamalākṣi kaṭākṣyatām ayaṃ
samayo varṇanayā rasārdrayā /
jana eṣa vacas tavāmṛtaṃ
śravasā pāyayituṃ kutūhalī // MV 7.40 //

"O lotus-eyed one!
Make this moment visible for me
by the description full of subtle feelings.
This man is eager to drink with his ears
the nectar of your speech."

iti sā dayitena bhāṣitā
daranamraṃ dadhatī mukhāmbujam /
vadati sma śanaiḥ śucismitā
sarasodārapadāṃ sarasvatīm // MV 7.41 //

She slightly lowered the lotus of her face
and slowly, with a bright smile,
she pronounced the speech
in measured cadence and effecting the sentiments.

She calls herself Kampana's *priyā*. The word *priyā* first of all means "beloved", "mistress", although a wife can be called *priyā*, too. Kampana addresses her using a very popular epithet 'lotus-eyed' and calling himself '*jana*', a name which can mean the person nearest to the speaker, a lover. She starts her recitation with a bashfully lowered face and delicate smile on it. Such a scene tells of the intimacy between the speakers but does not prove Gaṅgā's position as the lawful wife. She does not even add the second part to her name, *devī*, which could be treated as the title of a queen, princess or any woman of high rank.[22] Certainly, she shows herself as a talented poetess and a beloved of the king. Definitely, the image which emerges from her poem is not that of the chief queen and the number one in the king's harem. In fact, what she cares about is to show us an image of a well-educated and gifted poetess.

2.2. Royal poetess's education and talent

First of all the author is very much concerned to show how well she is familiarized with the Sanskrit language, theory of literature and the works of great Sanskrit writers. She not only mentions the greatest poets from the past but devotes to each of them one stanza in which she characterizes the style and language of a particular *kavi*.

In the strophe devoted to Bhāravi, she expresses such an opinion about his literary legacy:

vimardavyaktasaurabhyā bhāratī bhāraveḥ kaveḥ /
dhatte vakulamāleva vidagdhānāṃ camatkriyām // MV 1.9 //

[22] In the colophons -*devī* is added to the name Gaṅgā but they could have been written by a scribe. Additionally, some courtesans were also addressed with that *honorificum*, e.g., Mācaladevī.

Just like the garland of *bakula*[23] flowers
yields its scent when pressed,
so the composition of Bhāravi in close contact
reveals its beauty and fills the learned with awe.

Gaṅgādevī's list of Sanskrit *kavis* starts with Vālmīki and Vyāsa, then in chronological order the names of Kālidāsa, Bāṇa, Bhāravi, Daṇḍin and Bhavabhūti appear. Daṇḍin receives the title of *ācārya*. These great masters of yore definitely gained pan-Indian fame. The poets mentioned later are connected with South India. The poet of the *Karṇāmṛta* is praised by her in the following words:

mandāramañjarīsyandimakarandarasābdhayaḥ /
kasya nāhlādanāyālaṃ karṇāmṛtakaver giraḥ // MV 1.12 //

Whom would the words of the *Karṇāmṛta* poet fail to delight?
The words which are like an ocean of honey
which oozes from the flower clusters of the *mandāra*[24] tree.

The *Karṇāmṛta* poet is an almost legendary personage and many scholars have been trying to find out the truth hidden behind a great number of different legends about him.[25] It is believed that the *Kṛṣṇakarṇāmṛta* was written by Līlāśuka Bilvamaṅgala but there is an agreement among scholars that the text is of South Indian origin. It has its different versions and one of them comes from Bengal. It is said that the text was brought by Caitanya

---

[23] *bakula*, m. (also *vakula*) is a medium-sized tree, *Mimusops elengi*, said to put forth blossoms when sprinkled with nectar from the mouths of lovely women. Its small sweet scented flowers are white with a yellowish tinge. The fragrance remains even when the flowers are dried. So garlands made of *bakula* flowers are known as sweet smelling and durable.

[24] The Indian coral tree, *Erythrina variegata*, which according to mythology is one of the five heavenly trees.

[25] More in Introduction to the edition of the *Kṛṣṇakarṇāmṛta of Līlāśuka Bilvamaṅgala* (Wilson 1975).

c. 1510 from his pilgrimage in South India and it is an authoritative work for the followers of Caitanya in Bengal. Gaṅgādevī provides the earliest date for this poem.

Tikkaya is the next name given by the poetess. It must be one of the greatest Telugu poets, Tikkana Sōmayāji, who lived in the thirteenth century[26] at the court of Kākatīyas. He was one of the 'trinity of poets' (*kavitrayam*) who translated the *Mahābhārata* into Telugu. The other poets she mentions are her older contemporaries. These are: Agastya, a poet at the Pratāparudradeva II court at Warangal, then possibly under patronage of Bukka I; his nephews Gaṅgādhara,[27] a dramatist; and finally Viśvanātha.[28] Agastya is called by Gaṅgā the author of seventy-four poetic compositions, of which we have been able to trace only three works so far: a prose poem (*gadyakāvya*) the *Kṛṣṇacaritam*, the *Nalakīrtikaumudīkāvya* and an epic poem (*mahākāvya*) the *Bālabhāratam*. Gaṅgādhara is called the second Vyāsa as he dramatized the story of *Mahābhārata*. Agastya, Gaṅgādhara and Viśvanātha were connected with Pratāparudradeva II. His court seems to have been busy with men of letters; it is said that there were about two hundred poets there. He was also a scholar and a poet himself. We should stress firmly that in this way **Gaṅgādevī gives a picture of cultural continuity provided by the Sangamas: at the courts of Bukka I and his son these poets were respected and their works admired**. No wonder that

[26] If we belive that Gaṅgādevī's order is a chronological one, we have to agree that the author of the *Kṛṣṇakarṇāmṛta* lived after the eighth century, as this is the date for Bhavabhūti, and the thirteenth century is the upper limit, as he should be a prior or older contemporary of Tikanna.

[27] About this family connections read in Introduction to the edition of the *Bālabhāratam* text by K. S. Ramamurthy.

[28] Viśvanātha calls Agastya his maternal uncle (*mātula*) in the *prastāvanā* to his *Saugandhikāharaṇa* (see: Introduction to the *Kṛṣṇacaritam* by T. Venkatacharya, pp. VII–VIII and the *Saugandhikāharaṇa śl.* 4, ed. Sivadatta & Kasinath 1902: 2).

such an attitude could give rise to the later Telugu works such as the *Pratāparudra Caritramu* and the *Rāyavācakamu*, showing the greatness of Vijayanagara and implying that the Kākatīyas were actually the lineal predecessors of the Vijayanagara monarchs.[29] Gaṅgādevī's couplet dedicated to Viśvanātha allows us to presume that this poet was especially close to Gaṅgā. Perhaps he was her preceptor. She calls him the lord of poets and wishes him long life:

ciraṃ sa vijayībhūyāt viśvanāthaḥ kavīsvaraḥ /
yasya prasādāt sārvajñyaṃ samindhe mādṛśeṣv api // MV 1.16 //

May the lord of poetry, Viśvanātha, prosper long!
Through his favour, omniscience
has been lighten up even in someone like me.

A poet in South India, especially in the *cāṭu*[30] tradition, was believed to be omniscient as his talent was considered to be a divine gift. Velcheru Narayana Rao and David Shulman in their book *A poem at the right moment: remembered verses from premodern South India* retold some of the stories showing this amazing quality which discerns the greatest poets and always helps them win any kind of competition or solve a literary riddle.

The quoted stanza suggests that our poetess aspired to the position among the first rank poets, those who are omniscient. On the other hand, to prove that her knowledge of theory of literature is more than sufficient, she commences the discussion on theoretical issues. Some of her remarks, in fact, could be treated as her excuses addressed to literary critics. She says that, in reality, a perfect composition does not exist and critics should notice

[29] This line of reasoning will finally bring the works connected with the personage of Vidyāraṇya, such as *Vidyāraṇyakṛti* or *Vidyāraṇyavṛttānta*, in which the story about the service of Sangama brothers Harihara and Bukka under Pratāparudradeva II appears.

[30] More about *cāṭu* in footnote 38.

the merits of the work instead of concentrating on their quest for faults.

kvacid arthaḥ kvacic chabdaḥ kvacid bhāvaḥ kvacid rasaḥ /
yatraite santi sarve 'pi sa nibandho na labhyate // MV 1.17 //

In one (composition) there is (a quality of) sense,
in another (that) of sound, or *bhāva*, or *rasa*.
But nowhere is a work found
in which all these exist together.

guṇaṃ vihāya kāvyeṣu duṣṭo doṣaṃ gaveṣate /
vaneṣu tyaktamākandaḥ kāko nimbam apekṣate // MV 1.20 //

A villain leaving behind good qualities
searches for faults in poetic compositions.
The crow looks for *nimba*[31] fruit
disregarding the mangos in the groves.

Gaṅgādevī, anticipating perhaps possible accusations of plagiarism, or just revealing her views on the subject discussed in the circles of literati at her times,[32] openly declares:

cauryārjitena kāvyena kiyat dīvyati durjanaḥ /
āhāryarāgo na ciraṃ ruciraḥ kṛtrimopalaḥ // MV 1.21 //

How long can a villain play
with poetry acquired by stealing?
The counterfeit jewel is radiant
but the artificial colouring is short-lived.

Concluding her poetic manifesto, Gaṅgādevī once again suggests that her poetry is worth listening to:

---

[31] *Azadirachta indica*, its small olive–like fruit is bitter with one or two seeds, whereas the mango tree produces large, sweet fruit.

[32] For the opinion on this subject formulated by Bilhaṇa, see his *Vikramāṅkadevacarita* I.11 and I.12; also Bronner 2010: 461–462.

na prārthanīyaḥ satkāvyaśrutyai sahṛdayo janaḥ /
svādupuṣparasāsvāde kaḥ prerayati ṣatpadam // MV 1.24 //
tan madīyam idaṃ kāvyaṃ vibudhāḥ śrotum arhatha/
madhurāvijayaṃ nāma caritaṃ kampabhūpateḥ // MV 1.25 //

> A connoisseur needs no invitation to listen to good poetry.
> Who urges the bee to taste the sweetness of flower juice?
> Oh, learned men, deign to listen to that poem of mine
> entitled the *Conquest of Madhurā*, the story of king Kampa.

Also in stanza 7.40, as was noticed above, we are able to find confirmation that Gaṅgā is listed among the best poets at the court of Kampana, who himself is introduced as surrounded by good poets and a connoisseur of good poetry (MV 5.11).

In that way Gaṅgādevī presents herself as a well educated person suited to the company of great Sanskrit poets and continuing certain literary traditions. It must be admitted that such lengthy expositions[33] on a part of male authors occur quite rarely. It is a common practice that poets list a few of the names of their predecessors, which is a kind of a 'routine procedure' to pay homage to great ones, perhaps with the hope that they will be able to join the line of famous *kavis*. There are also poems authored by men which are completely deprived of such openings. It seems that the Vijayanagara poetess felt that she must give an immediate proof of her capability of being a writer.

One can agree that after reading even a part of her poem no other proof is needed. The *mahākāvya* authored by her is elegant

[33] In fact, among Gaṅgādevī's predecessors Bilhaṇa in his *Vikramāṅkadevacaritam* proudly shows off his knowledge of the theory of literature in as much as twenty-one stanzas (VC 1.9–29). Some of his couplets are similar in tone to those authored by our poetess, as for instance those concerning the wicked tracing faults and overlooking qualities (VC 1.20, 29). However, he does not list famous poets of the past, not to mention his contemporaries. He concentrates more on the presentation of his own person and literary skills, whereas Gaṅgādevī demonstrates herself as a competent theoretician and historian of Sanskrit literature, not so self-confident as her colleague-poet living in the eleventh century.

and its language correct from the grammatical and poetical point of view.

Her royal queen status, however, remains doubtful. Leaving aside the question of the position of Gaṅgādevī at Kampana's court, let as inspect the *mahākāvya* devoted to the exploits of Kampana in search of historical data and also traits which could be specific to women's writing.

2.3. Pregnancy, childbirth and family life in Gaṅgādevī's poem

Such physical conditions as pregnancy and childbirth are frequently mentioned in epic poems as they are important for the continuation of royal lineages. Even the definitions (*lakṣaṇa*) of a *mahākāvya* list the birth and raising of sons among the elements obligatory for this genre.[34] There is nothing exceptional in selecting such developments, however, as will be shown, Gaṅgādevī's presentation is quite unique.

Canto 2 opens with information about the pregnancy of Bukka's queen—*garbham adhatta devī*—and finishes with the stanza in which Bukka with his three sons is compared to Śiva with three eyes. The whole 42-couplet-long chapter is devoted exclusively to pregnancy, childbirth and raising children, but Gaṅgā speaks more about feelings connected with those issues than rituals and ceremonies, which are of main interest for male writers. In thirteen stanzas she describes Devāyī's pregnancy mentioning all the signs which prophesy the future greatness of the infant. These were: eating the particles of earth and other adventurous and unusual whims, such as bathing in the Tāmraparṇī river although the Tuṅgabhadrā was flowing nearby (MV 2.5). In the first stage of pregnancy, the queen's slender body and pale face is compared

[34] e.g. Daṇḍin, *Kāvyādarśa*, 1.17 ... *kumārodayavarṇanaiḥ*.

to the *śara* grass[35] (MV 2.2a). Next comes the comparison of the pregnant woman to the autumnal river with its water lilies closing by the end of the day but reflecting the moon during the night.[36] Obviously, the child in the mother's womb is compared to the moon but also the mythical lineage of the Sangama dynasty is alluded to.[37] Then the poetess describes the physical changes in the appearance of the pregnant woman informing about the king's positive reactions to them:

kramāj jahadbhiḥ kraśimānam aṅgair
mukhena mugdhālasalocanena /
madhyena ca tyaktavalitrayeṇa
nareśvaraṃ nandayati sma rajñī // MV 2.9 //

The king rejoiced over the queen
with the limbs of her body gradually forgetting thinness,
her face with charming and languorous eye-looks
and the waist no longer possessing three folds.

saubhāgyagandhadvipadānalekhā
rarāja tasyā navaromarājiḥ /
tejonidhiṃ garbhatale nigūḍhaṃ
kāloragī rakṣitum āgateva // MV 2.10 //

A fresh line of hair on her abdomen,
this stroke of ichor connecting her with happiness,
was glittering as if it were
a black female snake come to protect
this treasury of glory hidden in her womb.

śyāmāyamānacchavinā mukhena
stanadvayaṃ tāmaraseksạṇāyāḥ /
saṃdaṣtanīlotpalayor abhikhyāṃ
rathāṅganāmroraḍharīcakāra // MV 2.11 //

---

[35] *Saccharum sara or munja Roxb.*, a very large tufted grass, pale straw coloured, with long white hairs. Its white flowers are of ornamental value.

[36] *vilūnarājīvavanā dinānte chāyāśaśāṅkena śarannadīva//* MV II.2

[37] The genealogical tables of Sangamas show the Moon as their progenitor.

Both breasts of the lotus-eyed,
with the nipples growing dark,
were surpassing in beauty a pair of *cakravāka* birds
with blue water-lillies (in their beaks).

tām ambugarbhām iva meghamālāṃ
velām ivābhyantaralīnacandrām /
antastharatnām iva śuktirekhām
āpannasattvāṃ prabhur abhyanandat // MV 2.12 //

The king was delighted with her carrying the foetus,
as if she were a rain-cloud pregnant with waters,
a pearl oyster with a jewel inside
and the evening hour hiding the moon inside.

The picture of the pregnant queen, on the one hand, refers to the conventional description of a beautiful woman so often met with in *kāvya* literature, on the other hand, it truly depicts the stages of pregnancy. First the queen loses weight, becomes pale and shows different longings of a pregnant woman. Then she puts on weight. Then comes the conventional delineation of different parts of her body. The breasts are compared to the *cakravāka* birds (*Tadorna ferruginea*, the Ruddy Shelduck), which are usually found in pairs and their body plumage is light-brown. That is why two breasts are so often compared to the birds living in pairs and attractive in colour. The nipples were growing darker with the progress of pregnancy and they are compared to the darkest among Indian flowers, namely dark blue water-lilly flowers. The contrast between the dark nipples and light skin of the breasts was stressed by the poetess. The line of hair coming from the deep navel was always depicted and admired by the poets. In the case of a pregnant woman the depth of the navel cannot be accented because of physical changes. That is why Gaṅgādevī concentrates on the hairline which is compared to a dark snake. It is a female snake, which is also worth noticing, that guards the unborn child. The belly of a woman considered to be a beauty should be adorned with three folds. Again, it is not possible for a pregnant lady, but there are other charms the expectant queen shows off: sweet glances and plumpness. And what is stressed—she was attractive to her husband. The child in her womb is compared to white objects: a pearl, waters and moon, a fact which foretells a great future for him.

The last stanza (MV 2.13) in this long description of a pregnant woman, full of sophisticated comparisons, informs us that the king celebrated the *puṃsavana* ceremony accordingly to the prescriptions given by his *purohita*.

After announcing the birth of an infant (MV 2.14), the poetess, in 11 consecutive couplets, shows the reaction of the world, or better to say that of the universe, to this event. First we can see the shining quarters as if newly washed by the royal fame of the milk ocean whiteness. A cool breeze scented by the pollen of heavenly trees blew gently, the god of fire seemed to dance in joy in expectation of the sacrifices which would be performed in all southern countries and the *kalpa vṛkṣa*, the wish-fulfilling divine tree, was showering down flowers. Now we are moving to the animal world: wild elephants trumpeted in joy as if feeling a premonition that the infant would grow up to be a lion hunter; horses neighed with joy in expectation of the moment when the prince would mount them. Then finally this happiness came down to the world of men. The king's subjects celebrated the moment with blowing trumpets and bards (*cāraṇa*) chanted memorable verses (*cāṭu*).[38] The king was overwhelmed with joy, ready to

[38] In Sanskrit *cāṭu* means 'pleasing words', *cāṭu* verses, however, create a whole system and they live in the oral context. "Once an existing poem (for instance, from a classical source) enters this system, it is transformed in highly specific ways; poems created within *cāṭu* tradition naturally embody its particular understanding of poetry, the poet's role and power, and metaphysics of language proper to this system. The mode of transmission and elaboration is entirely oral; once *cāṭus* are collected and recorded in manuscript or printed books, they belong to a different stage of literary history and mean something

give himself to those who brought the happy tidings (*avāñcchad ātmānam api pradatum*—MV 2.22). He also decreed that:

viśṛṅkhalās tasya girā nirīyuḥ
kārāgṛhebhyo vimatāvarodhāḥ /
tuluṣkabandīnivahāya tūrṇam
āgāmine dātum ivāvakāśam // MV 2.23 //

The offenders were unchained
and left the prisons by his order,
as if to quickly make room
for the future mass of Tuluṣka prisoners.

Such a reaction by the king is in complete agreement with the *Arthaśāstra* prescriptions recommending the release of prisoners on the occasion of the birth of a male child:

(...) *putrajanmani vā mokṣo bandhanasya vidhīyate* // AŚ 1.36.47cd
(...) or when a son is born (to the king), the jail is emptied.

Then together with Bukka we are able to see the newborn: his two reddish hands, gracefully shaped feet, all the auspicious marks on his body, his large eyes like lotus petals, his lofty nose and red lips adorned with a smile. This detailed depiction from toe to top (in Skr. *nakhaśikhāvarṇana*, i.e. from a toe-nail—*nakha*—to *śikhā*—a lock of hair on the crown of the head) consists of six strophes (MV 2.25–30). Parental feelings and emotions overwhelmed Bukka. Tears of joy appeared and he embraced the child with his eyes. The king's emotions were clearly recognizable due to horripilation (MV 2.31–32).

---

different. Usually *cāṭu* verses are ascribed to highly visible poets and associated with narratives about them" (Rao, Shulman 1998: 135–136). Perhaps the poetess stresses the fact that the bards were true masters in their art adding grandiose splendour to the celebrations so these verses were remarkable and worth memorising.

The technique of the description adopted by the poetess makes the lying-in-chamber the centre of the universe; not only the chamber—it turns out that Vijayanagara ruler's court is in fact the centre of the universe. The eyes of the gods, animals and people are focused on it.

The dominating colour is white again:

snātas tato dhautadukūladhārī
vitīrya bhūri draviṇaṃ dvijebhyaḥ /
mahīpatiḥ putramuhkhaṃ didṛkṣuḥ
prāvikṣad antaḥpuram āttaharṣaḥ // MV 2.24 //

The king bathed and clad in white fine robes.
After disposing of immense riches to Brahmanas,
wishing to see the face of the son,
he sped to the gynaeceum, overjoyed.

avaikṣata kṣāmaśarīrayaṣṭeḥ
kumāram utsaṅgagataṃ sa devyāḥ /
śaratkṛśāyā iva śaivalinyās
taraṅgalagnaṃ kalahaṃsaśābam // MV 2.25 //

He saw the boy lying on the lap
of the weak and slender-bodied queen,
like a goose nestling on the waves
of an autumnal river reduced in waters.[39]

prakīrṇakāśmīraparāgagaurais
tiraskṛtābhyāntaradīpaśobhaiḥ /
nivāryamāṇaṃ muhur ujjihānair
ariṣṭagehaṃ mahasāṃ prarohaiḥ // MV 2.26 //

The lying-in-chamber was incessantly protected
by the rays of light,
whitish as the scattered saffron dust
and surpassing the lustre of the lamps.

---

[39] Autumn comes after the rainy season and is described in *kāvya* poems as white in colour and with the waters coming back to riverbeds.

To that white and shining picture, the poetess adds strokes of reddish colour: the small hands of the newborn forming fists again and again had the colour of fresh shoots (*muhurmuhuḥ pallavapāṭalena muṣṭikṛtena dvitayena pāṇyoḥ*—MV 2.27ab); it was pleasant to look at his little fingers similar to delicate, reddish new leaves (*pravālatāmrāṅgulidarśanīyau*—MV 2.28 c); and reddish was also the colour of his lips (*tāmrādharoṣṭham*—MV 2.30c). The tinges of red can speak about love as this colour represents passion and love as well.

Due to the talent of the author and perhaps also the fact that it was a woman-writer who created these passages, the reader clearly senses the intimate atmosphere of the emotional scene between husband and wife welcoming the newborn child.

The child was brought up by trustworthy nurses, but Bukka watched every stage of the child's development with joy and interest: his first tottering gaits and the lisping words.

The contact with the little one was a source of immense pleasure for the king:

tadānanaṃ tasya sugandhi jighrann
ālakṣyadantāṅkuradarśanīyam /
na tṛptim āsādayati sma rājā
navodayaṃ haṃsa ivāravindam // MV 2.37 //

The king never had enough of kissing[40]
the fragrant mouth of the child
with no teeth noticeable in it.
Just like a *haṃsa*[41] bird is never satisfied
with sniffing at the budding lotus.

---

[40] The word used here for kissing comes from the root *ghrā* and means a sniff kiss, i.e. the touch of the lips and nose usually on the head (here evidently on the mouth), "smelling the family smell of one's child or other kin" (Smith 2005: 53). In *sarga* V, stanza 60, Kampana is shown with the ladies from his harem as he kisses them. This time the word *paricumbana* is used (derivatives based on the root *cumb* mean a kiss of the lips).

[41] More about the *haṃsa* birds or geese in: Vogel 1962.

tathā na karpūrabharair na hārair
na candanair nāpy amṛtāṃśupādaiḥ /
yathābhavan nirvṛtam asya gātraṃ
sutāṅgasaṃsparśabhuvā sukhena // MV 2.38 //

The pleasure his body derived
from touching the limbs of his son
was such that even the contact
with camphor, pearls, sandal paste and moon-beams[42]
cannot give it.

The next strophe shows both parents with their child:

kalakkaṇatkāñcanakiṅkiṇīkaṃ
gṛhāṅgaṇe jānucaraṃ kumāram /
ālokayantāv amṛtāmburāśer
magnāv ivāntaḥ pitarāv abhūtām // MV 2.39 //

Both parents, looking at the prince
crawling on all fours in the house's courtyard,
with small gold bells tinkling,
were as if submerged in the ocean of *amṛta* nectar.

The author of this canto depicted the aspects of family life in a particularly touching way, showing the affection of a husband to his pregnant wife and the parental feelings towards a newborn baby. It is done from a woman's perspective as if the poetess herself was this pregnant woman, then the one in childbirth, who wanted to make her husband happy and proud because of the birth of a son. Of course there are conventional and unavoidable elements in this description, such as the mention about proper ceremonies of *puṃsavana*, *jātakarman*, *nāmakarman*[43] and the omens

[42] According to the conventions observed in *kāvya*, all the listed items are cool and extremely pleasant in contact. Additionally, all of them are white in colour.

[43] Among three prenatal and five childhood *saṃskāras* or the rites of passage, only these four are mentioned in the *Madhurāvijaya*: *puṃsavana*—a rite

and auspicious marks on the child's body, but it is not the characteristic feature of this chapter or *sarga*. What really is essential here and makes this canto exceptional within the realm of Sanskrit poetry are the scenes from the life of a woman presented with all poetical skills. The poetess did her best to make the audience able to visualize the scenes which took place in the private apartments of the royal couple. In fact, in this particular moment it is not so important that this is a royal couple. We have a man, a woman and a newborn boy before our eyes. She mentions colours, fabrics and uses sophisticated comparisons and metaphors which help imagine the situation. Due to skilfully applied alliterations, we are able to hear the jingling of the small gold bells ornamenting the limbs of the crawling prince. The imagery in this canto is very successful.

If, for the sake of comparison, we try to look at the poems written by male writers, Gaṅgādevī's predecessors, it is essential to find such works which devote considerably long passages to pregnancy and childbirth. One of such works would be the *Vikramāṅkadevacarita* of eleventh-century poet Bilhaṇa, which is devoted to the rule of Vikramāditya Tribhuvanamalla, who reigned at Kalyāṇa from 1076 to 1127. The poet describes in detail the queen pregnant with her second child Vikramāditya (VC 2.60–79). Bilhaṇa speaks about the pale face of the queen (VC 2.60), her resemblance to the *kandalī* tree, the flowers of which are white (VC 2.61), and a lot of attention is given to the breasts of the woman (VC 2.63–66)—they are compared to golden pitchers[44] containing fragrant nectar for the prince and the nipples are in fact two

performed during the second, third or fourth month of pregnancy in order to beget a male child, *jātakarman*—a rite meant for the development of the intellect of the newborn child, *nāmakarman*—the name-giving ceremony performed on the 12th day after birth, and additionally, in the first stanza of chapter III, *caula* or *cūḍākaraṇa*, a tonsure ceremony performed in the child's third and fifth year, is referred to. More about these *saṃskāras* in: Pandey 1969.

[44] It quite often occurs in *kāvya* that female breasts are compared to pitchers or jars.

dark leaves of invigorating herbs for him. Thus such an utilitarian treatment is far from evoking emotions of the kind described in the *Madhurāvijaya.* We also learn that the folds of skin disappeared from her belly. The stanzas mentioned here are created on the basis of complicated metaphors and comparisons and the rest of the passage is even difficult to comprehend. Even if the happiness of the king is mentioned here and there (VC 2.62, 77, 79), we do not have a feeling that the eyes of the king are focused on his beloved. He happily and eagerly awaits his second male child, who, as was foretold, will be the greatest among his three sons and that is why he appreciates all signs which show that this moment is close. Then the description of the lying-in-chamber (*sūtikāgṛha*) is given. The chamber was duly prepared by the experienced ladies who scattered rice for protection of the child and supplied drugs recommended by the physicians. Armed men were standing near the threshold of the house with protective plants. The people of the town were uttering incantations.[45] This picture resembles very much the lying-in-chamber of queen Vāsavadattā presented in the *Kathāsaritsāgara* of Somadeva,[46] a contemporary of Bilhaṇa, and a court poet of king Ananta, whom Bilhaṇa, a Kashmirian travelling all over India, also mentioned in the final verses of the *Vikramāṅkadevacarita* containing his own life-story. The moment of childbirth was announced by the drum of the lord of gods and divine flowers dropped from heaven. There is no description of the child—only the mention about his superhuman body (*... lokottareṇa vapuṣa ...*—VC 2.88). The king was happy because "in this world, indeed, it is the chief fruit of the life of householder" (*iha hi bhuvane gārhasthasya pradhānam idam phalam*—VC 1.91b). The descriptions we are offered in the two

[45] Such practices, at least some of them, can be still observed, especially in rural India; more about childbirth in India: Ram 2009, Naraindas 2009.

[46] *Kathāsaritsāgara* of Somadeva, Book IV: *Naravahanadattajanma.* Here one can find a description of a newly-born child although not so detailed as in the *Madhurāvijaya.*

mahākāvyas differ very much as to the contents and the way of their presentation.[47] In the *Vikramāṅkadevacarita* the emotions of the pregnant queen and the feelings of the husband towards his wife and the father towards his son are not shown. We see an important event for the king and his kingdom but the familial bonds and tender feellings are not shown here.

Perhaps the only work with which Gaṅgādevī's composition could be compared as far as the treatment of the subject of pregnancy and childbirth is concerned is the *Raghuvaṃśa* of Kālidāsa. The third canto of the *Raghuvaṃśa* opens with a sentence informing about the pregnancy of Sudakṣiṇā, desired by her husband and welcomed by her friends. The following stanzas inform not only about the desires of the pregnant woman and the changes in her appearance but also about the feelings of her husband. Although the news about the pregnancy made him happy, when in private he kissed her mouth, he could not attain satisfaction because of the smell of earth, which means that Sudakṣiṇā had been tasting particles of earth as her son was supposed to rule the kingdom[48] in the future. He enquired of her friends if she had a desire for anything. He was pleased (*nananda*—RV 3.11) seeing her putting on weight and moving with difficulty in order to greet him arriving at the residence. It turns out that couplet 12 of the *Madhurāvijaya* quoted above is based on the very same idea as stanza 9 of the *Raghuvaṃśa*:

---

[47] The sixteenth century historical *mahākāvya* the *Pāṇḍyakulodaya* gives a considerably long description of a pregnant queen (4.27–33) and the childbirth (4.33); however, these are again only the descriptions of the body of the mother-to-be, without any emotions shown. Also Rājanātha Diṇḍima, the author of *Acyutarāyābhyudaya*, in the first sixteen stanzas of canto II, describes the pregnancy of Acyuta's mother.

[48] *tadānanaṃ mṛtsurabhi kṣitīśvaro rahasy upāghrāya na tṛptim āyayau /* RV 3.3ab.

nidhānagarbhām iva sāgarāmbarāṃ
śamīm ivābyantaralīnapāvakām /
nadīm ivāntaḥsalilāṃ sarasvatīṃ
nṛpaḥ sasattvāṃ[49] *mahiṣīm amanyata* // RV 3.9 //

The king regarded the pregnant queen as reminding
the sea-clad earth with the treasure in its womb,
like the *śamī* tree[50] with fire concealed in it
or like the river Sarasvatī with its water hidden in the interior.

tām ambugarbhām iva meghamālāṃ
velām ivābhyantaralīnacandrām /
antastharatnām iva śuktirekhām
āpannasattvāṃ prabhur abhyanandat // MV 2.12 //

The king was delighted with her carrying the foetus,
as if she were a rain-cloud pregnant with waters,
a pearl oyster with a jewel inside
and the evening hour hiding the moon inside.

Close reading reveals the resemblance in the choice of the vocabulary, too. The underlined words can be found in the stanza of Gaṅgādevī almost in the same place in the verse.

Perhaps another one of Kālidāsa's stanzas was also an inspiration for Gaṅgādevī, namely the verse showing the pleasure of the king arising from contact with his child's skin:

tam aṅkam āropya śarīrayojaiḥ
sukhair niṣiñcantam ivāmṛtaṃ tvaci /
upāntasaṃmīlitalocano nṛpaś cirāt
sutasparśarasajñatāṃ yayau // RV 3.26 //

Having placed him (his son) on his lap,
whose skin was as if sprinkled with *amṛta*,

[49] The text commented by Vallabhadeva reads *sagarbhām* (Goodall, Isaacson 2003: 84), a word with the same meaning—'a pregnant woman'—and the same number of syllables, which is important for the metre.

[50] *śamī*—*Prosopis spicigera*, a small flowering tree possessing a very hard wood supposed to contain fire; it was employed to kindle the sacred fire.

the king, with his eyes closed at the corners
due to the pleasures arising from the contact
with (his child's) body, stayed aware of the delights
of the touch of his son for a long time.

The couplet describing the first lessons of walking and talking taken from the nurse (RV 3.25) also shows a picture similar to the one drawn by the Vijayanagara poetess.

There can be no doubt that Kālidāsa's strophes show the family bonds in a way not found in another male written poems;[51] however, the *Madhurāvijaya* offers more scenes like that, not omitting any moment important for a woman—starting from the first signs of pregnancy, showing the physical changes in the woman's body, then the delivery and the description of the newborn, mentioning not only auspicious signs but the real physical body of the child, and finally the visit of the father in the lying-in-chamber and his reactions in contact with the child. All these traits present in the whole second canto of the *Madhurāvijaya* speak of a woman's authorship.

There is also one stanza which should be mentioned here as it refers to the pregnancy and childbirth. The context in which it appears is quite unusual for such a subject:

antarbimbitacampendrā kampendrasyāsiputrikā /
apsarobhyaḥ patiṃ dātum antarvatnī kilābhavat // MV 4.81 //

Indeed, the sword of King Kampana
with the reflection of Sambhuvarāya in it,
was like his pregnant daughter
supposed to give birth to a husband for *apsarases*.

[51] The works of Kālidāsa are unusual and innovatory in many respects. It can be claimed, for instance, that the main character of his *mahākāvya* entitled the *Kumārasambhava* is in fact a heroine—Pārvatī, a very unique fact, indeed. More in: G. Tubb, "Heroine as Hero: Pārvatī in the *Kumārasambhava* and the *Pārvatīpariṇaya*" (Tubb 1984).

Of course it is a hint that Kampana's opponent, Sambhuvarāya, should be treated as a hero, as only the spirits of slain heroes are received and greeted with honours by celestial maidens. Nevertheless, the poetess designed a complicated metaphor aiming at childbirth.

2.4. Women at Kampana's court

It will be of great interest to see how and in which situations women are described in the *Madhurāvijaya* poem and if their presence occurs also in other contexts than the topics necessary for a *mahākāvya*. Of course the motif of the birth of a son/sons is naturally connected with a woman but it has been already discussed.

First of all, it must be stated that quite a lot of space is devoted to the depiction of the women at Kampana's court. These are queens, dancers and servants, too.

We see young women with jingling bracelets bearing chowris and standing on both sides of Kampana during official occasions of receiving monarchs ruling the neighbouring countries (MV 5.9–10). There are women dancers at his court, some of the ladies play the musical instruments and sing the panegirycs about his achievements (MV 5.12–13). As we know, some of them are even the authors of these eulogies and the king introduced as a connoisseur of good poetry appreciates their works. Of course, in the women's apartments there are maid-servants (*sairandhrī*), as is described in stanza 6.69, who help the king to dress properly. The world of all these women revolves around its central figure, namely the king. The monarch is the real centre of the women's universe. As we can imagine, the royal ladies appear in the parts of the poem which deal with the subjects meant to produce *śṛṅgāra-rasa* or erotic sentiment, as for example "play in the garden, playing in water, drinking wine and the delights of love-making" (KA–D. 1.16b: (…) *udyānasalilakrīḍāmadhupānaratotsavaiḥ*). Indeed, we see the king who "like Indra always attended by celestial nymphs" goes with his ladies to the garden to gather flowers.[52]

Such a sentence opens canto 6 dedicated to the garden pleasures, among which frolicking in the water takes the most prominent place. The ladies following the king move to the accompaniment of sounding jewelled girdles and anklets (MV 6.2, 5). Their glances are compared to blue and white water lilies and red lotuses[53]—a very appropriate comparison as the subject of garden with an indispensable element of garden landscape, namely the pond, is going to provide the background to the scenes presented in this *sarga*.

Interestingly enough, we are able not only to see the beautiful women forming the colourful and shining retinue of the king, we can also overhear their conversations.

If we think about the internal structure of a *mahākāvya*, it consists of descriptive and discoursive passages.

---

[52] *atha varatanubhiḥ samaṃ kadācid*
viracayituṃ kusumāpacāyalīlām /
pramadavanam amartyakāminībhir
harir iva nandanam āsadan narendraḥ // MV 6.1 //

One day thereafter
the King set out to the pleasure grove
to pass the time in picking flowers
with his graceful queens-
just as the noble Indra sets out for his garden Nandana
with heaven's beauties.

(transl. Ramarajan & Kotamraju 2013: 67)

[53] As is well known, whenever the colour of the eye is mentioned in Sanskrit poetry, the poets speak not about the iris but the pupil and the white. The contrast between the dark pupil and the clear white of the eye is stressed. Gaṅgādevī follows this pattern. In MV 6.4 she speaks about glances radiating dark and white hues, which reminded the darkest among Indian flowers, i.e. blue water lilies (Skr. *kuvalaya*) and white water lilies (Skr. *kumuda*). The red hue in the eye could speak about love passion. The eyes of a fierce warrior would be described as red in colour.

However, the speeches in court poems are mainly devoted to statecraft.

Another element indispensable for a *mahākāvya*, one of politico-military sequence, namely the counsel, is just ideal for showing the orators and present the *nīti* subjects. And these are men who debate about statecraft. Very often the speeches of women in the epic court poem, such as those of Draupadī in the Bhāravi's *Kirātārjunīya* or those of Vibhīṣaṇa's mother in the *Bhaṭṭikāvya*, not to mention Rati's lament in the *Kumārasaṃbhava*, originate from the *vilāpa* subgenre of epic poetry.[54]

The women in the *mahākāvya* world do not speak too much. And cerainly it happens very rarely that they speak among themselves. They are to embellish the epic court poem in the same way as they adorn the royal court—with their presence, perfect bodies and their charm. Here we observe an unusual trait for a *mahākāvya*—we are able to hear their courteous small talks. They pay compliments to each other comparing their feet to lotuses (MV 6.8), shining finger-nails to water (MV 6.9) and their faces to a lotus (MV 6.10). They show protective care trying to caution their co-wives against the pearls from broken necklaces on the paths, which could injure their delicate feet (MV 6.7), and they give advice to each other (MV 6.11). An ideal king, his ideal women in the ideal world of *kāvya* created by a woman-writer. Was it wishful thinking of a woman belonging to a highly formalised world, in which also emotional expressions were subordinated to routines, and her longing for such a court at which there was no place for any intrigue and no envy between the co-wives? Or can we trace a subtle irony in such verses as stanza 8:

nalinamukhi na bodhaya prasuptān
iha maṇinūpuraśiñjitena haṃsān /
drutagamanavighātam ācareyur
niyatam amī tava pādapadmalagnāḥ // MV 6.8 //

[54] More in: Viswanathan Peterson 2003: 58–63, Pigoniowa 2005.

"Oh, lotus-faced lady!
Don't wake up the geese which are sleeping here
with the sound of your jewelled anklets!
They would cling to your feet like lotuses
and prevent you from hurrying ahead."

Is this admiration for beautiful feet and graceful movements of one of harem damsels, causing the anklets to jingle sweetly, or is irony hidden here: 'that one is always trying to be the first'. Anyway, the conversation is very polite and the women seem to pay compliments to each other.

Contrary to such a presentation, we find other *kāvyas* abounding in depictions of envious women at courts of kings. In the *Vikramāṅkadevacaritam* of Bilhaṇa, an epic poem which could have influenced Gaṅgādevī's own writings, there is the kind of conversation between women (VC 12.23–29). Each of the stanzas is full of caustic remarks concerning the behaviour of the rival-ladies:

asaṃśayaṃ nīlasaroruhākṣi
samāruroha tvayi pañcabāṇaḥ /
drutair viniryāsi padair yad eṣā
kaśāhatevottaralā turaṅgī // VC 12.26 //
asmākam ālokanvighnahetos
taraṃgitāṅgī purataḥ sthitāsi /
kiṃ tuṅgavātāyanasaṃgatānāṃ
karoṣi mātsaryaparā parāsām // VC 12.27 //

"Oh, lady with eyes like blue lotuses,
the five-arrowed god (i.e. Cupid) doubtlessly got upon you
because you are going out with quick paces
like a trembling female horse struck with a whip.
You, with your body having folds,
are staying in front for the obstruction of our sight.
Being jealous, what will you do to other ladies
who are at elevated windows?"[55]

[55] Banerji & Gupta 1965: 197–198.

Such malicious words of rivalling ladies were heard to the amusement of king Vikramāditya.

Unfortunately, the next stanzas from the courteous conversation at the Kampana's court are missing[56] and the rest of this interesting talk is not available to us. The poetess continues with the conventional presentation of frolicking in the water of the king and his women. If we are going to accept the picture presented by Duarte Barbosa, Portuguese officer and traveller and the author of the so-called *Livro de Duarte Barbosa*, it will not only be a conventional picture so often met with in *kāvya* literature but also a testimony to certain habits of the Vijayanagara kings. Barbosa mentioned that the city abounded in tanks, in which beautiful courtesans bathed daily and the king went to see them doing so, and the one who pleased him most was sent for to come to his chamber (Barbosa 1.208).

The scene showing the pleasures of outing finishes with the stanza aptly closing it:

atha viharaṇakhedamantharābhiḥ
saha niragāt saraso nṛpaḥ priyābhiḥ /
kalaśajalanidher ivāpsarobhir
vibudhatarur mathanaśramālasābhiḥ // MV 6.66 //

Then, the king emerged from the pond
together with his beloved ones
fainting because of the fatigues of outing.
He resembled the tree of gods
surfacing from the milky ocean
with the *apsaras*es languorous
due to the exertion of churning it.

Then the company went to women's apartments (*śuddhānta*), where the king could admire the view of the ladies tying their

[56] The text from stanza 14 up to *śloka* 56 of this chapter is incomplete.

hair and redressing (MV 6.68[57]). He, too, was helped by maid-servants to put his royal garment on and, after worshipping Śiva, he attended to his duties for the rest of the day (MV 6.69[58]).

Such presentation of intimate situations in the king's harem can be also found in connection with as popular a theme in *kāvya* literature as the depiction of the seasons (*ṛtuvarṇana*). The descriptions of the seasons contained in the *Madhurāvijaya* are in fact the depiction of royal damsels throughout the year and their amourous adventures with the king during summer, monsoon season, autumn, winter and spring. The wintertime descriptive passage as a whole is satiated with *sambhogaśṛṅgāra*.[59] Each and every stanza shows the charms of royal ladies in wintertime and the king involved in acts of love with them. The other seasons are designed as landscapes with the royal women. After presenting the season, there are always remarks about the attractive look of

---

[57] *cikuraniyamaneṣu kāminīnām*
abhinavavastraparigrahāntareṣu /
abhimatapadadarśanair ayatnair
atimadanaṃ svam amaṃsta kamparājaḥ // MV 6.68 //

King Kampa considered himself above God of Love,
because he could easily feast his eyes on
his beloveds while they were changing into new cloths
and were having their hair done.

[58] *tataḥ sairandhrībhiḥ kṛtasamucitākalparacanaḥ*
purandhrībhiḥ sārdhaṃ samadhigataśuddhāntavasatiḥ /
trayīgītaṃ tejastripuraharam ārādhya vidhivad
yathārhair vyāpārair narapatir ahaśśeṣam anayat // MV 6.69 //

Then the maid servants put proper ornaments on him,
and together with his queens he entered women's inner apartments.
After worshiping Śiva, accordingly to the rules,
whose glory is sung by the Vedas,
the King for the rest of the day
attended to affairs deserving his attention.

[59] *sambhogaśṛṅgāra*—a variety of *śṛṅgārarasa* showing 'love in union' in opposition to *vipralambha* — 'love in separation'.

the king's ladies arousing his love passions. In summertime their faces are adorned with pearl-like drops of sweat and the *śirīṣa* flowers[60] placed on the ears (MV 5.21). The beads of sweat inform not only about the summer heat but they can betray a woman's sexual desire:

madanasaṃbhṛtagharmapayaḥ kaṇair
bhṛśam alajjata mugdhavadhūjanaḥ // MV 5.59cd //

The newly wedded young women
with sweat of love passion
collecting (on them) in drops
were very much ashamed.

Perhaps the same message is contained in the verse describing the king's wives during the spring festival:

kṣitipatiṃ kila kuṅkumamuṣṭinā
samabhitāḍayituṃ dhiyam ādadhau /
sapadi gharmapayaḥprasareṇa taṃ
vigalitaṃ na viveda vadhūjanaḥ // MV 5.75 //

The women intended to throw
a handful of saffron at the king
but indeed,
they did not realize that immediately
it had vanished with the excess of sweat.

Then again we find the stanza describing women's amorous feelings revealed by perspiration:

ma[em.; *m** Ed.]*danavera*[corr.; *bera* Ed.]*ni[bhaṃ] nibhṛtaṃ puraḥ*
kṣitipatiṃ kṛtacandanacarcikāḥ /

60 *śirīṣa* (*Acacia lebbeck*, Willd.)—flowers in summer and it very often appears in depictions of this season of the year; however, it also symbolizes the fair complexion of a woman and her delicacy.

adhikagharmapayobhir avāgaman
mṛgadṛśo vikasatpulakaiḥ karaiḥ] // MV 5.72 //

The fawn-eyed women
applying the sandal paste
with their hands (marked with) horripilation
and excess of sweat
revealed their secret before
the king with a Madana[61]—like body.

In contrast with Western aesthetic notions of sweating, in India this function of the body was traditionally known and appreciated as a visible symptom of sexual interest and arousal, and quite often mentioned by the poets.

The description of an autumnal night contains a beautiful comparison of it to the royal damsels:

vilasad utpalalocanaśālinīḥ
sphuritacandramukhīḥ kumudasmitāḥ /
narapatiḥ sphuṭatārakahāriṇīr
niraviśad dayitā iva yāminīḥ // MV 5.47 //

The king enjoyed the autumnal nights
which resembled his beloved ones with eyes like blue water lillies,
faces like the glittering moon, smiles like white water lillies
and the clear whites of their eyes like the stars.

To sum up: the way in which Gaṅgādevī pictures the royal ladies is not realistic at all. It seems that there is no envy between the king's women, no rivalry between the co-wives and all of them are well-disposed towards one another. It is not easy to believe such a picture. Of course, we cannot expect the realism to be a priority in *kāvya* literature, although the theoreticians of Sanskrit literature speak about such a quality of literary composition (*bhāvikatva guṇa*); elaborated style and sophisticated figures

[61] Madana, Kāma—the god of love.

of sound and sense as well as nice descriptions are more important. However, in this case there is a 'realistic' explanation to the fact: she herself belonged to this circle of royal ladies and, as such, she was not willing to criticise the relationships among the king's women, especially if she was not the first one among those damsels. Even the images believed to be conventional in such a case could be interpreted wrongly and made the other women ill-disposed towards her. Definitely, the ranking and etiquette were strictly observed among women living in separate palaces or quarters (*antaḥpura*),[62] but in this particular court poem or at least in what has come down to us, we are not able to identify the most important among Kampana's wives and establish Gaṅgādevī's position in this hierarchy.

[62] The *Kāmasūtra* informs how the senior (*jyeṣṭha*) and junior wives (*kaniṣṭha*) should behave towards one another (KS 4.2.1).

Chapter 3
Between Historical Truth and Dynastic Legends
Translating Literature into Memory

As was already said, one cannot expect realism from *kāvya* literature; nevertheless, in the patron-centred *mahākāvya*, which come into fashion in the eleventh century, there are always important pieces of information, despite the fact that the storyline is sometimes even fantastic.

Let us see what the Vijayanagara poetess says about the Sangama dynasty and Kampana, the hero of her composition.

3.1. Bukka I—the founder of the dynasty lineage

The *Madhurāvijaya*'s hero is Kampana, the son of Bukka I, and his victory over the Sultanate of Madura, as the title stresses, is the main theme of this particular literary work. Nevertheless, the poem starts with the eulogy of Bukka in 27 stanzas (MV 1.26–43 and 1.67–75). It could not be any different as it was Bukka who appointed his son a viceroy. Moreover, he, in fact, was the real creator of the Sangama dynasty. It seems that in the beginning, each of the five sons of Sangama ruled over his own territory and there was no absolute sovereign. After some time it was Bukka who gained the supreme position and his descendants formed the first lineage of Vijayanagara kings. Bukka Rāja is introduced in the *Madhurāvijaya* as a younger brother of Harihara (*hariharānuja* MV 1.26b). Harihara is not given the title of king here. So the role of the founder of the dynasty is ascribed to King Bukka. Also in the genealogy of the Sangama kings provided by the inscriptions, the name of Harihara I is omitted as was pointed out by T. N. Mallapa (Mallapa 1974: 35).

Bukka is described in the Madhurāvijaya in conventional terms as the tree of *dharma* (*dharmamahīruh*), his fame manifests as "sandal paste on the chests, as pearl earrings in the ears and camphor powder on the faces" (MV 1.31), and his right hand is "drawing the goddess of prosperity of his adversaries by her braided hair" (MV 1.35). Among all these conventional phrases, we find also statements which are fully confirmed by the epigraphical and archaeological evidence and other literary sources. Bukka is described as one "who counts on his arms as his only ally in the battle" (MV 1.29b: *bāhum eva raṇotsāhe yaḥ sahāyam amanyata*) and this is what we know from different other sources. Some sources claim that Harihara and Bukka started their career either at the courts of Kampiladevarāya and Kākatīya king Pratāparudra or according to other traditions, the brothers were in service with the Hoysala ruler Vīra Ballāla III.[63] No matter what was the beginning of their career, the truth is that in fact their own military talents, courage and cleverness granted them their own kingdom. Bukka's expertise in military science is also alluded to in the passage of the *Madhurāvijaya* devoted to the education of his son. Young Kumāra Kampana was educated in military sci-

[63] The epigraphical evidence contained in Vasundhara Filliozat's *L'épigraphie de Vijayanagar du début à 1377*, shows that the Sangama brothers started their career under the Hoysala king Ballāla III. The works such as *Vidyāraṇyakṛti* or *Vidyāraṇyavṛttānta* promote *the version* about the service of Sangama brothers Harihara and Bukka under Pratāparudradeva II.

ence by his own father, who gained it from an excellent masters (*tīrthalabdhāyudhavidā*—MV 3.2a).

The *Madhurāvijaya* is the only early source in which the name of Devāyī, Bukka's queen, is recorded (MV 1.43). In stanza 1.43 Bukka is introduced as a man "who acquired all his riches by the conquest"—*vijayārjitasampad*—and his capital is called the "City of Victory"—Vijayanagara, which serves here as the etymological explanation for the name of the city. Vijayanagara, or more precisely Abhinavavijayanagara, was mentioned as King Bukka's magnificent capital in the inscription dated 1368 for the first time. This inscription in poetical language introduces Śrīvīra Bukkarāja Śrīmanmahārajādhirāja Rājaparameśvara as the Lord of the Eastern, Southern and Western Oceans (*pūrvadakṣiṇapaścimasamudrādhipati*), who mounted the great throne of the new Vijayanagara, which is like the main jewel in the middle of the pearl necklace of the Tuṅgabhadrā River encircling the Hemakūṭa Mountain as if it were the neck of the lady Earth.[64] Earlier inscriptions give the names of some other cities as Bukka's seats: according to the inscription from Rāmapuram dated 1350 A.D., he was ruling from a place called Pūlipajeyapaṭa (Gopal & Ritti 2004: 42); in the inscription from the Kadiri (Anantapur District) dated 1352 Bukka was ruling in Penugonda and Dvārasamudra; in 1354 in the Penugonda inscription, Hosapaṭṭaṇa (other names: Virūpākṣa-paṭṭaṇa, Vijaya-virūpākṣa-pura, i.e. Hampi) is mentioned as the place from which Bukka ruled over the kingdom of the Hoysalas (Gopal & Ritti 2004: 53–54). In 1357 Harihara I died and the inscription of Bukka I for the first time gives the name of Vijayanagara (Filliozat 1973: 39). It is possible that Bukka I began the construction of a new city, his future capital, in that particular year. It seems

[64] *vasundharāvadhūkaṃṭhāyitahemakūṭādriparisarapariṣkāri-tuṃgabhadrodāramuktāhāramadhyanāyaka-ratnāyamānābhinava-vijayanagaramahāsiṃhāsanaśikharādhiroha (...)*
(*Epigraphia Carnatica*, vol. VII, Śikāripura 281, pp. 256–7; 332–5; translation: Vasundhara Filliozat, *L'Épigraphie de Vijayanagar du début* à 1377, p. 96).

that in 1368 the city was completed and became the capital of Bukka. The expression *abhinava vijayanagara* can refer to Vijayavirūpākṣapura, one of the names known from the Hoysala-period inscriptions describing Pampā/Hampi. In this case the *abhinava* epithet suggests that besides the older City of Victory dedicated to the god Virūpākṣa, there is a new city bearing the name of Vijaya. The Abhinavavijayanagara could have been situated on the grounds of the area identified presently as the 'Royal Centre'. The copper-plate grant dated 1378, to which Saletore refers (Saletore 1933: 105), mentions not a New City of Vijaya but the Supreme City of Victory (*vijatya viśvaṃ vijayābhidhānaṃ viśvottaraṃ yo nagarīṃ vyadhatta*). Again a very poetic description of the city is given:

> Its fort walls were like arms stretched out to embrace Hemakūṭa. The points of its battlements like its filaments, the suburbs like its blossom, the elephants like bees, the hills reflected in the water of the moat like stems—the whole city resembled the lotus on which Lakshmī is ever seated. There, with the Tuṅgabhadrā as his footstool, and Hemakūṭa as his throne, he (Bukka) was seated like Virūpāksha for the protection of the people of the earth.
> (Saletore: 1933: 105)

This interesting passage uses Puranic imagery employed for the general description of the world, which can be represented in the form of a lotus with mount Meru as its pericarp and the continents around it as its petals (Rocher 1986: 130, ftn. 86).

It can be noticed that the language of the inscriptions goes in pair with the growing importance of Bukka: very simple in the very first inscriptions, then more and more sophisticated and fitting in his figure into the image of a paramount king. Definitely, it is proof that King Bukka's court was becoming a cultural centre with poets able to present their monarch skillfully. And Gaṅgādevī was one of these talented poets at the court.

3.2. Gaṅgādevī's description of the City of Victory[65]

In the detailed description of the Vijayanagara as offered by Gaṅgādevī, besides the usual metaphors connected with the subject obligatory in the *mahākāvya*, namely the description of a city, one can find a great amount of information corroborated by the travellers and archaeological surveys. We learn that the river Tuṅgabhadrā compared to the heavenly Gaṅgā (*svarṇadī*), which flows round the borders of the city, makes its natural moat (MV 1.44); nevertheless, the city is also protected by ramparts as high as mountains. The high and gem-set *gopura*s resembling the peaks of Sumeru adorn the city (MV 1.46)—again an allusion to the fact that we are dealing with the image mapping the mythical landscape.

The inhabitants of the city could enjoy the beauty of the gardens (*ārāma*) which looked like abodes of Spring, full of different flowering ornamental trees, such as *campaka*s,[66] *aśoka*s[67] and

---

[65] Some parts of this subchapter directly connected with the description of the Vijayanagara city as well as some remarks concluding the whole chapter were published in my article "Vijayanagara City as Described in the *Madhurāvijaya* and *Acyutarāyābhudaya*", see: Sudyka 2010. The article shows Vijayanagara city as described by Gaṅgādevī in terms of an orthogenetic city in the sense proposed by Robert Redfield and Milton B. Singer.

[66] *campaka* (*Michelia champaka*)—an evergreen tree cultivated beacause of its white or yellow strongly scented flowers. The flowers are used in religious ceremonies and by women for decorating their hair. There is a belief that the tree flowers only if a young woman sprinkles it with perfumed water.

[67] *aśoka* (*Jonesia asoka* L., syn. *Saraca asoka* (Roxb.) De Wilde)—the tree is cultivated in many gardens because of its decorative orange red flowers and evergreen beautiful foliage; sacred for Hindus and Buddhists. It is connected with god of love being a symbol of love. There is a belief that it flowers when kicked by a beautiful young woman. *Aśoka* is one of the most frequently mentioned plants in Indian literature. More about *aśoka* in *kāvya* literature in Sudyka 2004a.

nāgakesaras.[68] There are pleasure hillocks (*keliparvata*) there, an idispensible element in Indian garden landscape. They are frequented by the musk deer (*kastūrīhariṇa*) looking for the shade of plantains[69] and camphor trees.[70] The sporting-lakes (*krīḍāsara*) with lotuses on them, inhabited by *kalahaṃsa* birds (*Anser anser*), with gem-set steps (*maṇisopāna*), are mentioned (MV 1.49). The steps of *dīrghikās* (MV 1.60) are also paved with gems (*mānikyamayasopāna*). According to Monier Monier-Williams dictionary, *dīrghikā* means "an oblong lake or pond". Here evidently the authoress describes artificially made water tanks, rectangular in shape. In the long tradition of Hindu India gardening, the idea of a garden is exactly the same as all over the world; three basic elements of water, a mountain and a tree constitute such a place.[71]

The elevated portions of the city have "high-built palaces, white like the clouds of autumn" (MV 1.50). The city palaces (*prāsāda*) are so high that their pinnacles (*śṛṅga*) are able to catch the disc of the sun (MV 1.55) and damsels playing on the top floor of the mansions "often laid their hands on the rounded body of the moon, mistaking it for their play-ball of pearls" (MV 1.56). The place where the ladies used to play the ball is called *candraśālā*. According to the information contained in the introduction to the *Śṛṅgāramañjarīkathā* by Bhojadeva, the *candraśālās* were special

[68] *nāgakesara* (*Messua ferrea*)—so-called Indian rose chestnut or Ceylon ironwood—is a big, ornamental tree with large fragrant white flowers.

[69] *kadalī* (*Musa sapientum* L.or *Musa paradisiaca* L.)—the plantain or banana tree, an evergreen tall plant with purplish brown drooping flowers, cultivated all over India, considered auspicious by the Hindus and used for religious ceremonies. Its stem is a symbol of frailty.

[70] *karpūra* (*Cinnamomum camphora* (L.) J. Presl)—an evergeen tree with yellowish white flowers in axillary panicles. Camphor, a white crystalline substance, is obtained from the tree.

[71] More about gardens as described in Sanskrit *kāvya* literature in Sudyka 2009.

apartments on the terraces, with white-washed walls and decorated with paintings, from which the moonrise was observed.[72] Because of these paintings they were also called *citraśālās*.

As one can notice, the white colour plays an important role in the palette used by the poetess. The city is described as having palaces white as autumnal clouds (MV 1.50), the city's sportive lakes are full of lotuses and white-feathered birds, in the gardens grow *campakas* and *nāgakesaras*, and camphor plants which have whitish flowers. Also camphor pigment and balm are white in colour. The faces of city damsels are lotus-like (MV 1.61). The ladies play with a pearl ball which is mistaken for the full moon. The city is always full of light even at nightfall due to the lustre of gems with which the steps leading to the lakes and palaces are set. That is why the *cakravāka* (*Tadorna ferruginea*)[73] birds can stay together during the night (MV 1.60). The white colour, images of light present in the city delineation, as we already know, belong to the *kāvya* repertoire and expresses the king's fame (*kīrti*), which is also white in colour according to colour symbolism present in Indian tradition. The capital city, as was said previously, is connected with kingship. So the Vijayanagara city, white and luminous, symbolises the rule of Bukka I, who himself gathers luminosity and becomes its earthly receptacle.[74] The same concept was employed in the above-discussed inscription from 1368, where

---

[72] Bhoja, *Śṛṅgāramañjarīkathā*, 1959, Intr. p. 80. The *Śṛṅgaramañjarīkāthā* provides a very interesting, colourful and abounding in different architectural details depiction of the city of Dhārā. Perhaps the most interesting are the descriptions of artificially watered public baths (*yantradhārāgṛha*) with many mechanical contrivances.

[73] There was a belief that *cakravāka* birds, due to a curse, have to spend the night in separation. That is why they are a symbol of love in separation.

[74] It is in accordance with Puranic vision of luminosity (*tejas*), the abstract force giving everything in the world the power to realize its destiny. The paramount rulers gathering and emitting light "might shine luminously in the entropic darkness of the Age of Strife" (Ali 2000: 204).

Bukka is introduced as ruling the city which is compared to the gem in the middle of the necklace, i.e. the river Tuṅgabhadrā.

This dominating white colour of the city, in the case of Vijayanagara as presented by Gaṅgādevī, is tinged with red and grey: among the trees blossoming in white, there appear *aśoka* trees. The geese on lotus ponds mentioned here are *kalahaṃsas*, which have white under- and upper-tail coverts, but their neck, body and wings are grey. *Rājahaṃsas* (*Anser indicus*) are much paler than the other breed and, in fact, the poets speak only about their white feather. Here the choice of poetess was for the *kalahaṃsas*. She mentions also musk deer and *cakravākas*. The general colour of musk deer coat is sandy brown. Also the *cakravāka* bird has orange and brown body plumage and a paler head. The wings are white with black flight feathers. The clouds which hang close to the palaces reflect *padmarāga* gems (i.e. rubies) lustre. That is why they always resemble the evening clouds coloured by the setting sun. Perhaps the selection of this palette is not fortuitous as these are the colours of physical surroundings of the Vijayanagara (Fig. 1). The Tuṅgabhadrā flows through a rocky terrain of pinkish-grey granite boulders (Fig. 4).

The expansive grounds of the city were inhabited by a crowd of virtuous Brahmanas, youths of fashion and beautiful women, as well as armies of musicians, informs Gaṅgādevī (MV 1.52, 53). Hearing the drums which accompanied the music played in the city mansions, the peacocks would dance although it was not the monsoon season. "Serenity and music reigned unceasingly all around" (MV 1.52b). Stanza 1.53b supplies us with the information about large number of people, perhaps visitors to the city, who "loved to wander in its precincts". In the evenings a dark cloud would hang over the city due to the smoke rushed from the buildings of the city (MV 1.59). There is no exaggeration at all in such a picture. We know quite a lot about the historical development of the city, which grew with extreme rapidity during the reign of Bukka I, first, due to several archaeological projects and systematic exploration of Vijayanagara and its surroundings and second, thanks

Figure 1: Vijayanagara surroundings. (Photo L. Sudyka)

Figure 2: Virupaksha Temple, Hampi. (Photo L. Sudyka)

Figure 3: Mahānavamī platform (Vijayanagara, Royal Centre), often identified as the place, from where the king witnessed the celebrations of the Mahānavamī festival. (Photo L. Sudyka)

Figure 4: Hampi, Tuṅgabhadrā River. (Photo J. Sudyka)

to numerous descriptions given by foreign travellers, who like the Italian traveller Nicolo Conti in the early 15th century or Abdul Razzaq Samarqandi, a Persian envoy visiting the city in the middle of the 15th century, or Athanasy Nikitin (d. 1472), a merchant from Tver, to name only a few of them, left detailed descriptions of the Vijayanagara city. There are also other literary sources giving a description of the city. Among them the *Saṃdeśarāsaka* by Abdul Rahman is of great interest. This Apabhraṃśa poem consisting of 223 stanzas can be situated on the borders of a message-poem (*sandeśakāvya*), although the term *rāsaka* refers to the *rāsa* composition popular in the old Western Rajasthani literature or the *rāsaka* genre associated with the worship of Kṛṣṇa. The author introduces himself as Addahamāṇa (SR 1.4), a weaver, son of Mīraseṇa from a famous Mleccha country in the west (*paccāesi puvvapasiddho micchadeso*—SR 1.3) and he possibly lived in the fourteenth century.[75] The name only betrays the Muslim origin of the author. It is not surprising that a Muslim poet writes[76] in vernacular and takes local genres:[77] it only proves the multiculturalism of the medieval Indian society. As to his social status, records of temple donations show that merchants and artisans were a very prosperous and important group in the Vijayanagara kingdom. King Kṛṣṇadevarāya, and definitely such an attitude towards encouraging trade and commerce in the kingdom was present long before his rule, declared in his *Āmuktamālyada*:

> A king should improve the harbours of his country and so encourage its commerce that horses, elephants, precious gems, sandalwood, pearls and other articles are freely imported (...). Make

[75] The commentary by Lakṣmicandra is dated 1409 by its author (Mayrhofer 1998: xii).

[76] It seems that this sophisticated poem was not composed orally. Its author shows himself as a well-educated person and one acquainted with Indian literary traditions and culture.

[77] See for instance: *Śṛṅgāramañjarī* of Saint Akbar Shah (Raghavan 1951).

> the merchants of distant foreign countries who import elephants and good horses attached to yourself by providing them with the villages and decent dwellings in the city, by affording them daily audience, presents and allowing them decent profits. Then those articles will never go to your enemies.
> (Rangaswami Sarasvati 1925: 69, 72)

King Kṛṣṇadevarāya speaks about imported goods, but Vijayanagara also exported some articles. Textiles were one of the most important exported products.[78] To demonstrate the high status of artisans, let us mention the Tamil community of weavers, known as Kaikkoḷas, who attained positions of responsibility at two important temples, Śrīraṅgam and Tirupati (Asher & Talbot 2006: 83). The increased strength of artisan communities, such as weavers and smiths, which started in the fourteenth century or even earlier, is revealed in the inscriptions.[79]

In the *Saṃdeśarāsaka*, the poem authored by a weaver, an unnamed heroine, a Vijayanagara city dweller, sees a traveller, and after learning that he is on his way from Multan (*mūlatthaṇu*—SR 2.65) to Cambay (*khaṃbhaittah*—SR 2.65, 67), she asks him to convey a message to her husband, who went on business to Cambay. She describes to him her feelings throughout the whole year of her husband's absence and in this way one can see some glimpses from Vijayanagara life from summer to spring.

Situated on the southern bank of the river Tuṅgabhadrā, Vijaya City was the capital of the Vijayanagara Empire from the second half of the 14th century to 1565. According to Carla Sinopoli,

[78] The richness of Vijayanagara fabrics, their different patterns and colours, are well attested by the preserved murals on the Lepakshi temple *raṅga-maṇḍapa* ceiling (see: Gopala Rao 1969; Kameswara Rao, V. 1982; Sudyka 2011).

[79] Noboru Karashima analyses the inscriptions from the North and South Arcot districts showing the development of trade and growing importance of artisan communities in his book *Towards a new formation: South Indian society under Vijayanagar rule* (Karashima 1993).

an archaeologist participating in the Vijayanagara Metropolitan Survey Project initiated in 1987, "it is not unreasonable to believe that populations may have been as high as 100,000 in the early 1400s, and more than twice that by the early 1500s".[80] In the first period of the city growth "the walls of the urban core were built and enclosed an area of approximately 12 sq km".[81] A dense centre of population required irrigation works, building tanks, water reservoirs and providing agricultural infrastructure. The excavations prove that during the initial period of the city growth, "agricultural communities and artisans were drawn to the region to serve the economic needs of the expanding urban population".[82] The identified residential sites "provide evidence for a mobile population that moved through the Vijayanagara region—including pastoralists, travellers, pilgrims, artisan and soldiers".[83] Over time the urban core expanded, incorporating the nearest settlements. The *Madhurāvijaya* offers a literary proof of this fact. In stanza 66 we have information that Pampā was a satellite town of Vijayanagara (*śākhānagarī*) and there was a temple of Virūpākṣa (Fig. 2) there and many wealthy lords resided nearby. As the story recorded in the sixteenth century, also by the Portuguese traveller Nuniz, has it, Harihara founded the temple of Pampāpati or Virūpākṣa (i.e. Śiva as the husband of the goddess Pampā) in order to honour his guru Mādhavācarya, otherwise known as Vidyāraṇya.[84] Today around the Virūpākṣa temple there is a village Hampi—the successor to the *śākhānagarī* Pampā. In fact this area, called the Sacred Centre, has its unbroken tradition of sanctity starting in the pre-Vijayanagara period. The Virūpākṣa temple was constructed on the foundation of earlier structures as

[80] Sinopoli 2004: 276, note 2.

[81] Ibid.: 268.

[82] Ibid.: 270.

[83] Ibid.: 275.

[84] Sewell 1992 (reprint): 300.

it probably existed long before the Vijayanagara period. However, it owes its present shape to the kings of the Vijayanagara Empire. It is still the centre of pilgrimages. Among the inscriptions coming from the eleventh to thirteenth centuries there is one registering gifts to the temple of goddess Hampādevī/Pampādevī. This local folk goddess identified with the Tuṅgabhadrā river was included into the Hindu pantheon by her marriage to Śiva as Virūpākṣa, then identified with Śiva's consort Pārvatī as her incarnation.[85] Hoysala-period inscriptions mention Virūpākṣapattana or Vijaya Virūpākṣapura.[86] Judging by the names of the locality, at certain time the cult of Virūpākṣa, the god worshipped in Karnataka,[87] became more popular there than that of Hampādevī. His presentation as a form of Śiva on the one hand, and the husband of the goddess of Tuṅgabhadrā river on the other, could serve a purpose of uniting local traditions and creating a chance for them to join the Great Tradition. In the fourteenth century the place protected by Śiva Virūpākṣa first became a large settlement as indicated by recent excavations, then a satellite town of the capital of Bukka I as presented by Gaṅgādevī, and later on a part of a huge urban complex.

Phillip Wagoner claims:

> It appears that by the opening of the 14th century, the tirtha at Hampi had become the pre-eminent ritual centre in the region, and

[85] It seems that very often the incorporation of the local goddess cult into mainstream Hinduism led through assimilating the particular goddess into the pan-Indian Śaiva tradition and including her into the Śaiva mythology as a wife or daughter of Śiva. Cf. Mīnākṣi mythology and her marriage with Śiva Sundareśvara; it is believed that Bhadrakālī cult offered possibilities of introducing local deities, together with specific ritual practices, into the pantheon of Hinduism and according to the myth popular in Kerala, Bhadrakālī originated from her father Śiva's third eye.

[86] Stein 1997: 31.

[87] Perhaps the oldest Virūpākṣa temple is in Pattadakal, the capital of the Cālukya dynasty. It was built in the 8th century.

> that the Sangamas' choice of this site for the construction of their new capital was consciously motivated by a desire to make use of the site's ritual power to legitimise their newly instituted kingship. Thus, when the city of Vijayanagara was laid out in the 14th century, it was the unoccupied plain to the south of the old pilgrimage centre that was built into an urban zone containing the royal palace, while the tirtha itself was transformed into a sacred zone for the city by the gradual construction of a series of royal temple complexes along the river and the extension of the city walls northward to bring this zone within their ambit. Through deliberate and systematic planning, the form of the new city functioned to effect a transferral of ritual authority from the old gods of the tirtha to the king who exercised it on their behalf from his palace in the royal centre.
> (Wagoner 1996a: 141)

All things considered, the description offered by Gaṅgādevī, though highly conventional, contains topographical and historical details, too.

There is tradition attributing the foundation of the city to Vidyāraṇya, and Vidyānagara, the alternative name of the capital city, could be seen as connected with this sage. But the early Sangama inscriptions connected Bukka I with the creation of the City of Victory, not mentioning the name of Vidyāraṇya in that context. Even the inscriptions of Harihara II, issued in the years 1380 A.D., 1384 A.D., and 1386 A.D., eulogising Vidyāraṇya make no reference to his role in the foundation of the city. There are certain early inscriptions referring to Vidyānagara, but the genuineness of these records was questioned by some scholars and other arguments opposing the idea of Vidyāraṇya's direct or indirect share in the building of the city and empire were given. According to these scholars, such as Heras, B.A. Saletore[88] and others, in Durga Prasad's words: "taking advantage of the weakness of the last Sangama rulers, the pontiffs of the Sringeri Matha

[88] Saletore 1936: 158–159.

fabricated and propagated these stories and even the inscriptions were deliberately forged by these gurus to highlight the Hindu religious fervour in the founding of the empire and the city."[89] Most recent scholarship by Herman Kulke and Philip Wagoner also denies the Sangama brothers close affiliation with this Hindu sage at the moment of building their kingdom.

In fact, the *Madhurāvijaya* authoress uses the name Vijayanagara exclusively and does not mention Vidyāraṇya at all. Instead she pays homage to Kriyāśakti, just after the invocation to Śiva, Pārvatī, Gaṇeśa and Sarasvatī, which commences her poem. She compares Kriyāśakti Guru, unparalleled in wisdom and shining with auspiciousness, to Śiva Trilocana with Pārvatī by his side.[90] It seems that Kriyāśakti, the *kula guru* of the Sangamas, as is known from the inscriptions, could be an influential and very important personage at the dawn of the city and the kingdom, while the influence and high position of Mādhava Vidyāraṇya started some years later,[91] perhaps in the last quarter of the 14th century as S. Thiruvenkatachari suggests in his *Introduction* to the edition and translation of the *Madhurāvijaya* text.[92] Hermann Kulke has also reached the similar conclusions that Mādhava Vidyāraṇya ob-

---

[89] Durga Prasad 1988: 198.

[90] *asādhāraṇasārvajñyaṃ vilasatsarvamaṅgalam /*
kriyāśaktiguruṃ *vande trilocanam ivāparam //* MV 1.4 //

> I praise Guru Kriyāśakti, who, like Śiva,
> is of extraordinary omniscience,
> and who shines with universal auspiciousness,
> like Śiva when he is with Durgā.

[91] It seems that there were different reasons for introducing versions of the Vijayanagara foundation myth into different texts as the case of the *Rāyavācakamu* proves. More about its textual strategies in: Ph. Wagoner, *Tidings of the King. A translation and Ethnohistorical Analysis of the Rāyavācakamu* (Wagoner 1993).

[92] Thiruvenkatachari 1959, Introduction, pp. 2–3.

tained the highest level of hierocracy only in his old age. Kulke also collected evidence showing that in fact there were two Mādhavas connected with the early Sangamas and belonging to two different families. The presence of Mādhavamantrin of Āṅgīrasa *gotra* and Mādhavācārya of Bhāradvāja *gotra* can be now treated as an established fact (Kulke 2001b: 208–239).

There is also another dissenting opinion concerning Vidyāraṇya and Kāśīvilāsa Kriyāśakti Deśika. According to T. N. Mallappa the inscriptions with the Vidyāraṇya's name were not fabricated at all and Kālāmukha Guru Kriyāśakti is Vidyāraṇya from the early Sangama inscriptions. After the consecration of his disciple Harihara II, he was addressed as Vidyāraṇya and

> (...) was installed as the first jagadguru of Sringeri matha, and it is from him the parampara of Sringeri jagadgurus starts. It is he who helped the formation of the Vijayanagara Empire through his disciples Madhavacharya of Angirasa gotra and Naraharimantri. (Mallappa 1974: 58)

The second Mādhava belonging to the Bhāradvāja *gotra* was the minister of Bukka. He was a brother of Sāyaṇa, the talented author of the *Parāśaramadhavīya*, but not such a great personage as Mādhava of Āṅgīrasa *gotra*, according to Mallappa. His arguments concerning the identification of Vidyāraṇya are presented in the book *Kriyasakti Vidyaranya*. As we know from the epigraphical evidence, contrary to the popular stories connecting the name of Śaṅkarācārya with the establishment of *maṭha* in Śṛṅgeri, the earliest reference concerning Śṛṅgeri only as the place of pilgrimages (*tīrtha*) comes from 1346.[93] In 1356 King Bukka donates villages to Vidyātīrtha and his disciples in Śṛṅgeri. Then the name of Vidyāraṇya does not appear in inscriptions at Śṛṅgeri until 1375. In the Śṛṅgeri *maṭha kaḍita* books (accounts), one can find an interesting story contained in the copy of Harihara II inscription and

[93] Śṛṅgeri inscription of Harihara I (Gopal & Ritti 2004: 8–10).

retold in Śṛṅgeri's *Guruvaṃśakāvya* composed in the 18th century. We learn that the senior guru Hiriya Śrīpadaṅga asked Vidyāraṇya to come back from Kāśī and on his return he ascended to the *gadī* of Śṛṅgeri. The title or epithet of Kriyāśakti describes him as "The Joy of Kāśī" (Kāśīvilāsa). Was it not Kriyāśakti, the *guru* of early Sangamas, who was asked to come back from Kāśī, then received the name of Vidyāraṇya and became the *mahant* of Śṛṅgeri *maṭha* and immediately Bukka I ordered Mādhavamantrin to grant lands to him? From that time the name of Vidyāraṇya occurs frequently in the Śṛṅgeri inscription and the *maṭha* receives generous support of Bukka I, then Harihara II.

Inscriptional evidence, however, is against Mallappa's concept that Kriyāśakti and Vidyāraṇya are one and the same person. The grant of Harihara II dated 1384 provides information that the king listened both to Kriyāśakti and Vidyāraṇya's teachings. A record from 1403 registers land grants both to Kriyāśakti-devarāya-voḍeyar and to the *guru* of Śṛṅgeri *maṭha* (Lorenzen 1972: 162). The identification of Mādhava belonging to Bhāradvāja *gotra*, a disciple of Vidyātīrtha, Bhāratatīrtha and Śrīkaṇṭha as Vidyāraṇya is also attested by his own literary works.[94]

Thus, as we can see, the debate concerning the identity of Vidyāraṇya was very vivid but it seems that finally convincing conclusions have been reached.

Judging by the opening of the *Madhurāvijayam* and what we know about the position of the *kula guru* during the rule of the first Sangamas, Kriyāśakti was an extremely important person in the kingdom of Bukka, more important than Mādhava or both Mādhavas and Sāyaṇa[95] as their names are not mentioned at all, and, what is more, Gaṅgādevī informs us that King Bukka relied only on his own judgement and power:

---

[94] "Mainly on the basis of this literary evidence of cross-reference in his own works, the traditional identification of Mādhavācārya can be considered an established fact" (Kulke 2001b: 226).

[95] About Sāyaṇa see in Galewicz 2009.

vivekam eva sacivaṃ dhanur eva varūthinīm /
bāhum eva raṇotsāhe yaḥ sahāyam amanyata // MV 1.29 //

He (Bukka) considered
his power of discrimination as his minister,
his bow alone as his guards,
and his arm as his only ally in the battle.

3.3. The Vijayanagara king as the saviour from the Muslim power

As mentioned before there are different accounts connected with the foundation of the Vijayanagara kingdom and city. Even if it is still a matter of controversy,[96] it can be safely stated that the beginnings of the Vijayanagara Empire are closely connected with the history of the Muslim expansion in the South of India. It does not mean, however, that the kingdom was founded in order to protect the Hindu culture and religion against Muslim invaders. The founders of the future empire, two brothers—Bukka and Harihara, were ambitious and intelligent chieftains who obtained the royal titles due to favourable circumstances created by the political chaos that followed the fall of older dynasties, such as the Hoysalas and Kākatīyas, and the appearance on the scene of the new and expansive power of Muslims. The military talents of the Sangama brothers and political situation enabled them to create a kingdom. Newly created kings and their realms require legitimization of rule and unquestionable authority behind them. Only then,

[96] According to research, particularly by Herman Kulke and Philip Wagoner, the Sangama brothers were most probably local warriors from Karnataka. They first served the Hoysalas. Then "they appear to have voluntarily given political allegiance to Muhammad Tughluq during the years when he was based at Daulatabad. Once Tughluq power waned in the Deccan, the Sangamas sought to establish their own state (...)" (Asher & Talbot 2006: 54).

at the stage of strengthening the Vijayanagara kingdom, did the time for preparing ideological background of consolidating value come. Building an empire involves composing or selecting a narrative that gives identity. The literature created at that time under the patronage of the newly established dynasty obviously served that purpose. And the *Madhurāvijaya* is the oldest literary document offering insight into ideological manipulations. The aim of a poet in service with the Vijayanagara monarchy must have been to show the power and greatness of the early Vijayanagara kings and all facts which could legitimate their right to the throne. Such traits are clearly visible in the *Madhurāvijayam mahākāvya* written by Gaṅgādevī, who was the wife/concubine of Kumāra Kampana, belonging to the second generation of the Sangama dynasty. The poetess first describes the defeat of the Sambhuvarāyas and establishing a prosperous rule in Kāñcīpuram. However, the reasons for the conquest of the neighbouring Tamil country are shown as preparations for the major task, that is the victory over Muslims. Here perhaps, for the first time, the image of the early Vijayanagara rulers as the protectors of Hindu *dharma* against Muslims appears. In canto 3 of the MV, king Bukka I explains to his son:

upetya tuṇḍīram akhaṇḍitodyamaḥ
pramathya campapramukhān raṇonmukhān /
praśādhi kāñcīm anuvartitaprajaḥ
patir nidhīnām alakāpurīm iva // MV 3.41 //

"You, making constant efforts,
after reaching Tuṇḍīra[97] country
and destroying those headed by Campa (Sambhuvarāya),
who only wait for war,
take care of the subjects and rule in Kāñcī
just like the Lord of Wealth does in the city of Alakā.

[97] Tuṇḍīra or Tuṇḍaka-viṣaya—a Sanskritized form of the name Toṇḍaināḍu or Toṇḍaimaṇḍalam, the historical region with Kāñcī as its capital.

athābhibhūtākhilavanyabhūbhṛtas
turuṣkabhaṅgas tava naiva duṣkaraḥ /
nigīrṇaśākhāśatasaṃ[vṛtaḥ? hatiḥ] kathaṃ
taruprakāṇḍaṃ na dahed davānalaḥ // MV 3.42 //

Then, if you subdued all the woodland kings,
it would not be difficult for you to break the power of Turuṣka.[98]
Would the fire that had devoured hundreds of branches
not destroy the trunk of a tree as well?

anena deśān adhikṛtya dakṣiṇān
vitanyate rākṣasarājadurnayaḥ /
tvayāpi lokatrayatāpahāriṇā
vidhīyatāṃ rāghavakarma nirmalam // MV 3.43 //

After imposing his supremacy upon the southern countries,
he exhibits the bad conduct of Lord of *rākṣasas*.
You should perform the virtuous deed of Rāghava,
reducing the affliction of the world.

The Sambhuvarāya chieftains of the North Arcot and Chingleput districts in Tamil Nadu rose to local prominence under the Colas. Then they were associated with the Pāṇḍyas and the most famous member of this family was at that time Kulaśekhara Sambhuvarāya (reign: 1306–1330), a son of Ekāmbaranāthan (Sethuraman 1987: 12). Upto 1322, according to epigraphical evidence, he was faithful to the Pāṇḍyas. In 1324 the Muhammadan army from Delhi ran in the Tamil country and occupied Madurai. The Pāṇḍyas fled to the northern areas of Tamil Nadu. Probably it was the weakness of the Pāṇḍyas which encouraged Kulaśekhara Sambhuvarāya to declare independence. As is attested by records, Kulaśekhara Sambhuvarāya and his son Ekāmbaranātha Venṟumaṇkoṇḍān Sambhuvarāya (reign: 1322–1339) successfully restored peaceful life in the Toṇḍaimaṇḍalam region of the Tamil country

[98] The words *yavana*, *pārasika* and *turuṣka/tuluṣka* are used as synonyms in the *Madhurāvijaya* meaning a 'Muslim' without differentiation of the origin of the invaders.

after the Muslim invasion under the leadership of Malik Kāfūr. They revived worship in the temples, took care of refugees and development of handicrafts. In 1337 Tirumallināthan Rājanārāyaṇa I, the elder son of Venṟumaṇkoṇḍān Sambhuvarāya, came to the throne and the following year his younger brother Poṉṉiṉ Tambirāṉ Rājanārāyaṇa II also started his reign. The territorial expansion of Bukka I and his son, presented in the *Madhurāvijaya* as a necessary and unavoidable prelude to a decisive battle with Turkish Muslims, put an end to the prosperity of the Sambhuvarāyas' kingdom.

Gaṅgādevī describes the Vijayanagara army—elephants, horses, foot soldiers—leaving the capital city, prince Kampana on his excellent horse,[99] with Cola, Kerala and Pāṇḍya monarchs as the staffbearers before him. To this picture the sounds of war drums, trumpeting of elephants and Brahmanas' chanting of Atharvaveda hymns augmenting the chances of victory should be added (MV 4.3–5, 16, 19). The cool breeze from the waves of the Tuṅgabhadrā welcomed the marching army. After five or six days of marching (*pañcaṣair eva vāsair*) through the Karṇaṭa country, Kampana with his army reached Kaṇṭakānanapaṭṭaṇa (MV 4.47), the modern Mulbagal or Mudlabāgalu, the city on the borders of Karnataka, Andhra Pradesh and Tamil Nadu. He stopped there for a while waiting for the appropriate hour to launch the attack against a Sambhuvarāya ruler. Kampana "struck camp near Viriñcinagara" (MV IV. 50), the modern Virinchipuram situated near Vellore. This time a breeze from the Dugdhavāhinī river, which is today called Pallar, is mentioned. After due preparations Kampana started to lay siege to Sambhuvarāya, who is called here a lord of Dravidas (*dramiḍādhipa*). It can be supposed that the siege of Viriñcinagara is alluded to in the text,

[99] The tall royal horse is described in ten stanzas (MV 4.20–29), which constitutes almost 1/4 of the whole *sarga*! To compare, the decisive battle between the two enemies takes only a few lines (MV 4.77–81).

but another possibility should be also taken into consideration, namely the siege of the town called today Padavedu. According to S.Thiruvenkatachari, the editor and translator of the *Madhurāvijaya* and the author of *Introduction*, Kampana besieged Kāñcīpuram (Thiruvenkatachari 1957: 33). I have not found any information confirming this supposition. It should be reasonable to suppose that the struggles must have taken place in the territory of the original home of the Sambhuvarāyas. The mention about a camp near Viriñcipuram and laying siege to Rājagambhīra make both towns—Viriñcipuram and Padavedu—more probable places of the events described in the *Madhurāvijaya* than Kāñcīpuram, which is situated circa 70 km from both Viriñcipuram and Padavedu (the distance between Viriñcipuram and Padavedu is around 20 km). Padavedu was the old capital of the Sambhuvarāyas. It is encircled by mountains and hills, where it was possible to seek shelter in case of defeat. And that was what the Draviḍa king did in fact, taking refuge in Rājagambhīra, a rocky fortress besieged by Kampana in all probability from Padavedu. According to the *Manual of the North Arcot District*, quoted by S.Thiruvenkatachari, Padavedu was once a large city full of temples. There were two forts upon the plains and another one upon the peak of the Javadi hills, overlooking the city (Thiruvenkatachari 1957: 68). Perhaps the latter one is the hill fortress the siege of which is described in the *Madhurāvijaya*. The town was conquered after fierce fights but the Tamil king's forces escaped and took shelter in the hill fortress named Rājagambhīra:

atha tasya purīm eva nītva śibiratāṃ nṛpaḥ /
acalaṃ rājagambhīram arundha dviṣadāśritam // MV 4.67 //

Then the king
converted his (i.e. Sambhuvarāya's) town into a camp,
and besieged the hill (fortress) Rājagambhīra
in which the enemy sought refuge.

It seems that Kampana began the siege of the fortress from the city which became his camp, and if so, it must have been a town at the foot of the Rājagambhīra hill. The sounds of his war-drums raised echoes from every hill cave:

taddundubhipratidhvānamukharaiḥ kandarāmukhaiḥ /
bhayād amandam ākrandam akārṣīd iva parvataḥ // MV 4.68 //

The mountain seemed to cry intensely
from fear with its mouth-like caves,
resounding with the echoes of his war-drums.

This sentence should be also treated literally as the area of Padavedu is encircled by mountains and hills. "The battle between the two armies again has started" (*atha pravavṛte yuddhaṃ sainyayor ubhayor api*—MV 4.70ab) and it was described as making the battlefield shining with the missiles falling and shooting up.[100] Is it an allusion to the use of artillery? According to the information provided by Mahalingam, in South India artillery was used for the first time in the battle of 1368 fought between Bukka I and Bahmani Sultan, which is attested by *Tohfut-us-Salaṭin* (Mahalingam 1967: 269–270). Perhaps the first usage of gun powder happened a few years earlier and thus was recorded by the poetess. As Burton Stein states:

> Reasons for the military success of Vijayanagara warriors against their Hindu and Muslim rivals are hardly considered in the existing literature on the Vijayanagara state. This is peculiar since all have differentiated the Vijayanagara state from others on the basis of its martial character and achievements. An unchanging dharmic

[100] *atha pravavṛte yuddhaṃ sainyayor ubhayor api*
patadutptadastrāṃśujvalitorvīnabhassthalam // MV 4.70 //

The battle between the two armies again has started,
lighting up both earth and sky
with beams of missiles
falling down and shooting up.

> ideology is presumed to account for the successes of the several dynasties; yet, as is clear from the records of Vijayanagara, the major victims of Vijayanagara military power were not Muslims but Hindus, and a major factor in this success were Muslim soldiers in Vijayanagara armies. (...) One that would appear to deserve serious consideration is that the success of Vijayanagara armies was a direct consequence of their experience with an imitation of Muslim armies, their tactics and weapon. (...) But there is another military factor which is almost totally ignored by Vijayanagara historians; that is the use of artillery by the Vijayanagara armies. (Stein 1980: 400, 402)

The fierce fight culminated in the duel of two kings described in four stanzas (MV 4.79–82). According to the relation of Gaṅgā, Sambhuvarāya was killed. One can suppose that Gaṅgādevī accompanied her husband in his raid,[101] but in fact there is no certainty if the whole campaign of the Vijayanagara prince was described faithfully in her poem. As Thiruvenkatachari observes in his *Introduction* to the edition of the *Madhurāvijaya*, if Kampana's invasion took place about 1351–2, a fact which is confirmed by the inscriptions,[102] and at that time Rājanārāyaṇa Sambhuvarāya was the ruler, how is it possible that we have Rājanārāyaṇa's inscriptions up to 1359? Who was then killed in the battlefield? Or possibly Sambhuvarāya was defeated and subdued but not killed. According to the epigraphical evidence convincingly presented by Thiruvenkatachari, Gaṅgādevī describes the second campaign against the Sambhuvarāyas. The first one took place in 1351–2 and as its result Rājanārāyaṇa accepted the supremacy of Vijayanagara.

[101] Duarte Barbosa says that the king of Vijayanagara ordered his men to take their wives and sons to the battlefield because "men fight better if they have the responsibility of wives and children and household goods on them" (Dames 1918: I, 225).

[102] There are about 132 inscriptions found in the districts of Chittoor, Chingleput, North and South Arcot, Tanjavur, Trichinopoly, Salem, Coimbatore and Ramanathapuram attesting to Kampana's conquest and rule in the Tamil country. The earliest one, dated 1352, is from Āvūr in the North Arcot.

According to Thiruvenkatachari, Kampana returned to the seat of his Mulbāgal Viceroyalty and spend the period between 1353 and 1359 there. However, there is an inscription from the Kōlar area dated 8th February 1356 informing that Bukka I appointed his son a viceroy of the Mulbāgalrājya "and entrusted him with the task of extending the Vijayanagara rule in the Tamiḻ country."[103] It is possible then that prince Kampana, after the first struggle with the Sambhuvarāyas, returned to his father's seat and only in 1356 moved to Mulbāgal. His cousin Vīra Sāvaṇṇa controlled the earlier subdued territory. Vīra Sāvaṇṇa and his general Sāluva Maṅgi both acquired the title of *sambhuvarāyasthāpanācārya*—another proof that the Sambhuvarāyas did not disappear from the scene in 1352 if Sāvaṇṇa and the general under Sāvaṇṇa were the "establishers of the Sambhuvarāya". These titles also point to the fact that actually the two warriors were the heroes of the first encounter of the Vijayanagara forces with the Sambhuvarāyas. According to Sethuraman's investigation based on a thorough study of the epigraphical evidence, the records of Rājanārāyaṇa II are available up to 1359 and his existence in 1359 is confirmed in the records of Rājanārāyaṇa III. Around 1362 there was a battle and possibly it was Poṉṉiṉ Tambirāṉ Rājanārāyaṇa II who was slain in it. Tirumallināthan Rājanārāyaṇa I surrendered to Kampana, who restored him to the throne, and we have his records from 1362. Later he figures as a donor in the record dated 1373 mentioning Kampana's name as a ruler. As Sethuraman concludes, he must have entrusted the affairs of the kingdom to his son Rājanārāyaṇa III, whose records upto 1375 are preserved. The fate of the Sambhuvarāyas after this date is not known.

It seems that the campaign against chieftains observing and guarding Hindu *dharma* was quite long and difficult. Should not the rulers of Vijayanagara, depicted as the protectors of the Hindu way of life, treat the Sambhuvarāyas rather as their allies belonging to the same league? Was not the campaign against the Hindu

[103] Srinivasan 1990: 83.

ruler a waste of time and power which should be directed towards Madurai Sultan immediately? The authoress tries to hide such an inconsistency on the one hand under popular sayings, such as: "Would the fire that had devoured hundreds of branches not destroy the trunk of a tree also?" (MV 4.42), as if the fights with the Sambhuvarāyas were a kind of exercise before the main task. Then under a picture of the heroic battle and Kampana's successful rule in the newly obtained country, a message is hidden that the rule of the Sambhuvarāyas was not in accordance with *dharma*:

ittham saṅgaramūrdhni campanṛpatiṃ nītvā kathāśeṣatāṃ
śrīmān kampanṛpeśvaro janayituḥ samprāptavāñ chāsanam /
kāñcīnyastajayapraśastir amithassaṅkīrṇavarṇāśramaṃ
nītyā nityaniratyayarddhir aśiṣat tuṇḍīrabhūmaṇḍalam // MV 4.83 //

In the field of battle,
having thus procured Campa to become a story only,
venerable king Kampana received a decree of his father
that he should rule (the territory thus conquered).
With the fame of his victory duly established in Kāñcī,
he inaugurated a just and prosperous rule over Tuṇḍīramaṇḍalam
destroying all confusion in castes and religious orders.

That is how Gaṅgādevī finishes canto 4. The sentence justifies the military action and on the other hand confirms the opinion that Vijayanagara was, at the beginning of its history, more a military confederacy of "many chieftains cooperating under the leadership of the biggest among them" (Nilakanta Sastri 1964: 79) than one kingdom. The Mulbāgal Viceroyalty now extended to Kāñcīpuram was actually ruled by Kampana himself. The next chapter offers the description of a happy life in the 'Emerald City' (Marakatanagara, i.e. Kāñcī). It seems that Kampana was not in a hurry to destroy the demoniac Suratrāṇa at all. He enjoyed a peaceful and pleasant life in Kāñcī for quite a long time, forgetting about his mission long ago entrusted to him by his father.

Gaṅgādevī's poem was written only after the Madurai victory and from the perspective of the victorious party. No wonder that the motives of the Sambhuvarāyas' campaign could be changed accordingly to the new ideology connected with the purpose of removing the Suratrāṇa from the political stage of Tamil Nadu and introducing Vjayanagara rule. It might also be, as Sethuraman suggested, that the Pāṇḍyas facing two serious problems, namely threatening power of the Madurai Sultanate and the strengthening position of the Sambhuvarāyas, asked king Bukka I for help. The fact which corroborates this opinion is that the Pāṇḍyas are described as Kampana's allies in the campaign against the Sambhuvarāyas, although it is highlighted by the author that they were staff-bearers for Kampana accepting his superiority completely. Secondly, the Vijayanagara kings brought Tamil Nadu under their control but the Pāṇḍyas were independent. After Vijayanagara victories they "retired to Ramnad, Tirunelveli and Kanyakumari districts. The Pāṇḍyas existed till the middle of the 17th century." (Sethuraman 1987: 21).

3.4. Kumāra Kampana—a picture of a son, husband and ruler

It seems that the name Kampana was quite popular among the early Sangamas. The younger brother of Harihara I and Bukka I was named Kampaṇa (or Kampaṇṇa) and also two sons of Bukka I bore that name. The two brothers were known as Hiriya Kampaṇa (i.e. older Kampaṇa) and Cikka Kampaṇa (i.e. younger Kampaṇa).

The table given below situates the hero of Madhurāvijaya among the family of the early Sangamas:

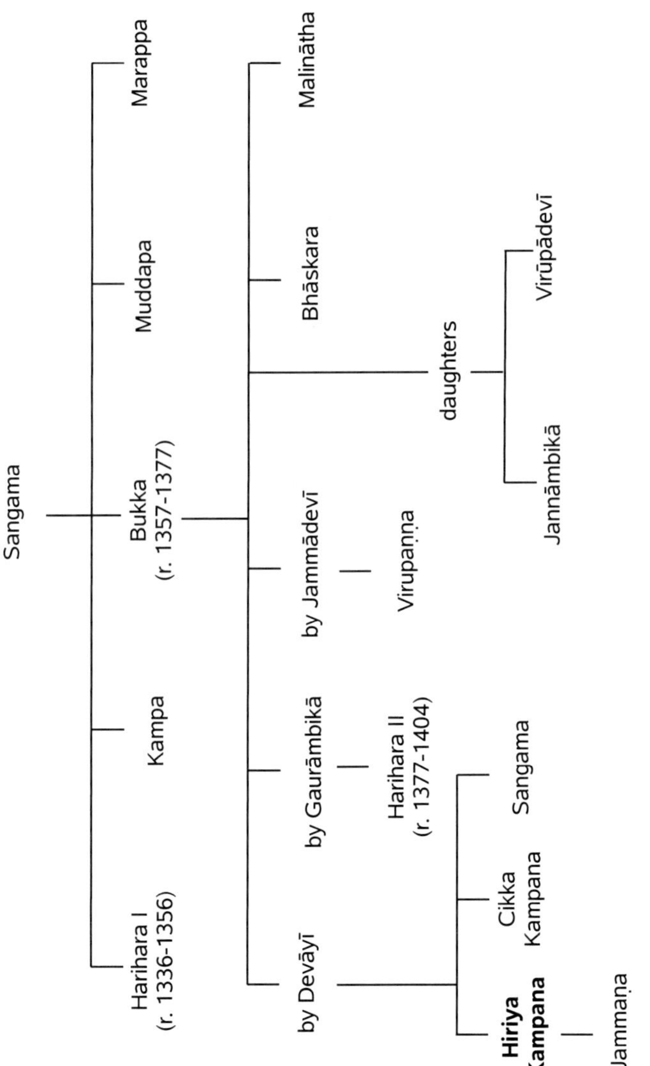

Table 1: Kampana's Lineage

M.B. Emeneau explains that the name Kampaṇ(ṇ)a is formed of the personal name Kampa and the Kannaḍa kinship term 'aṇṇa' —'elder brother'. Gaṅgādevī uses the form Kampa, calling her King Kamparāja, Kampanṛpa, Kampeśvara, Kampendra, Kampanarendra, Kampamahīpati, etc. Only once does she employ the form Kampana[104] while giving an ethymological explanation to that Sanskritized form of a Dravidian name:

ākampayiṣyaty ayam ekavīraḥ
saṃgrāmaraṅge sakalān arātīn /
ity eva niścitya sa dīrghadarśī
nāmnā sutaṃ kampana ity akārṣīt // MV 2.34 //

The (king), being far-seeing, felt assured that
this son would be a matchless warrior
and would cause all his enemies to tremble [verb stem *ā-kampaya-*]
on the field of battle, and named him Kampana.[105]

As M.B. Emeneau notices, the poetess must be "an accomplished Sanskrit scholar, and this verse is an echo of the epic passage in the *Mahābhārata* 2.4.19f–20".[106] The *śloka* from the MBh to which Emeneau refers reads:

(...) *kampanaś ca mahābalaḥ* // 19 //
satataṃ kampayām āsa yavanān eka eva yaḥ /
yathāsurān kālakeyān devo vajradharas tathā // 20 //

'and the mighty Kampana, who, all by himself,
ever made the Yavanas tremble [verb stem kampaya-],
as the thunderbolt-wielder Indra did the Kālakeya demons.'[107]

It introduces the famous *kṣatriyas* who gathered in Pāṇḍava's

[104] I use the Sanskritized form of the name, i.e. Kampana not Kampaṇ(ṇ)a.

[105] Emeneau's translation; Emeneau 1985: 401.

[106] Ibid.

[107] Ibid.

assembly hall, among them Kampana, who alone was able to make the Yavanas tremble.

One could agree with Emeneau that it must be a reference to the passage from the *Mahābhārata* and admire the education and skills of the poetess. It is worth mentioning that, at the same time, it suggests that it is also our Kampana's fate to make the Yavanas tremble. As mentioned earlier the ethnic terms such as *yavana*, *pārasika* and *turuṣka/tuluṣka* were designates of Muslims.

Bukka's queen gave birth to her son at an auspicious moment, as it pronounced by astrologers (*praśaste divase samastair mauhūrtikar sādhitapuṇyalagne*—MV 2.14a). She is compared to Pārvatī delivering a child to Śiva. All signs prophesied the great future of the first-born son of the royal couple: the gentle breeze was spreading the fragrant flower-dust from heavenly trees (MV 2.16), the flowers of *kalpa vṛkṣas* were falling down through the clouds (MV II.18), the auspicious circles described by dancing flames of the fire betokened that fruitful sacrifices would be performed all over the southern countries (MV 2.17). The quarters shone as if washed by royal fame comparable because of its whiteness to the milky ocean (MV 2.15). The living creatures in the kingdom were overwhelmed with joy. Interestingly enough, the poetess lists here only elephants, horses and people, as if to show that her prince will be a great commander of the Vijayanagara army who will lead the cavalry, infantry and elephants towards future victories. After giving the list of all good omens, Gaṅgādevī describes the festivities in the city. However, it could not be Vijayanagara city. Prince Kampana's campaigns into the northern Tamil country started in the 1350s as the inscriptions testify. It means that he could have been born in the 1330s, i.e. before his father established his capital known as Vijayanagara and acquired the position which Gaṅgādevī describes in the first chapter of her poem. Nevertheless, we can accept the picture of a town celebrating the birth of a male-child of its ruler[108] as is shown by the poetess: auspicious horns were sounded (*maṅgalatūrya*—MV 2.21), wandering singers (*cāraṇa*) were chanting the memorable verses (*cāṭu*) and people were in the joyous mood. Bukka wanted to give everything, including himself, to the messengers who brought the glad tidings. On his command prisons were emptied as if he could anticipate that quite soon space to hold Muslim prisoners would be needed (MV 2.23). After disposing great wealth to the Brahmanas, the king bathed and dressed in white silk entered the queen's apartments in order to see the face of his son. The scene which we are presented with is depicted by Gaṅgādevī in the white colour as she, as was said earlier, aims at suggesting prosperity and royal fame of the Sangama House, now increased by the birth of the prince. We see the king dressed in white silk (*dhautadukūla-dhārin*), his wife's lap is compared to the bank of an autumnal river and the newborn son to a duckling (*kalahaṃsaśāba*). Rays of light, white as camphor, played on the child's auspiciously marked body. On a proper day the *jātakarman* rites were performed by a priest, a name was selected for the child and the prince grew, tended by trustworthy nurses (*dhātrī*). The overjoyed King Bukka witnessed his son's first lessons in walking and talking. He liked kissing and embracing the little boy.

Soon the first-born child of the royal couple had two more brothers—younger Kampana and Sangama—and the princes grew together.[109] After the tonsure ceremony (*caula*), the prince became

[108] In the 1330s Ballāla III gave both talented brothers, Harihara and Bukka, special privileges, such as issuing records independently and using some of the titles (Srinivasan 1990: 81). Of course, to call Bukka at that time a king would be an exaggeration. Gaṅgā, however, starts writing her poem when Bukka was really a powerful ruler. Even if there were still people who remembered him in Hoysala service, her task was to present him as a king enveloped in all royal splendours.

[109] Bukka I fathered more sons but Devāyī must be his chief queen or this is the picture presented by Gaṅgā. In the Penugonda inscription of Bukka I dated 1354, it is said that he entrusted Penugoṃḍe-rājya to his son, Virupaṇṇa,

proficient in all arts and sciences. Under the guidance of his father, he acquired perfection in martial arts. As Gaṅgādevī says the qualities of all the Pāṇḍava brothers: Yuddhiṣṭhira, Bhīma, Arjuna, Nakula and Sahadeva were gathered in this one person:

sa satyavāg bhūribalo dhanurdharas
turaṅgam ārohaṇakarmamarmavit /
kṛpāṇavidyānipuṇaḥ pṛthābhuvām
adarśi saṃghāta ivaikatāṃ gataḥ // MV 3.3 //

> He was truth-telling, immensely strong, proficient in archery,
> knowing the tricks of mounting a horse,
> conversant with knowledge of swordplay.
> One could see all (accomplishments) of Pāṇḍavas united.

So this time the *Mahābhārata* and its main heroes are used by the poetess in order to create a picture of Kampana's valours.

Then the poetess gives a detailed depiction of the youth (MV 3.6–16):

sa sarvataḥ parvatakandarāśrayaiḥ
parigrahānugrahakāṅkṣibhir gajaiḥ /
vitīrṇam utkocatayeva dhīradhī-
-radhārayad vibhramamantharaṃ gatam // MV 3.6 //

> His gait was entirely dignified and graceful,
> as if (with it) this clever-minded one
> were bribed by the elephants
> dwelling in the mountain caves
> and longing to be caught and kept (by him).

sa rūpagarveṇa nirāsthad aṅghriṇā
smarasya nūnaṃ jayavaijayantikām /

born of the queen Jommādēvi (Gopal & Ritti 2004: 53–54). After the death of Bukka I, his and Gaurāmbikā's son, Harihara II, ruled between 1377 and 1404. Bhāskara and Mallinātha or Mallappa were also the sons of Bukka I. Among Bukka's daughters Jannāmbikā is mentioned (Rice 1909: 112) and Virūpādēvi (EC X.10; EI: 232, 285).

na cet katham̩ tasya tale 'tikomale
sulekham ālakṣyata mīnalāñchanam // MV 3.7 //

Indeed, he must have put his beautiful foot
on Kāma's banner of victory.
If not for that, why the auspicious lines
on his soft sole form a sign of a fish?

śubhākṛtes tasya suvarṇamekhalaṃ
kaṭisthalaṃ sthūlaśilāviśaṅkaṭam /
vyaḍambayan nūtanadhātupaṭṭikā
-pariṣkṛtām añjanabhūbhṛtas taṭīm // MV 3.8 //

The loftiness of the buttocks of this handsome (young man),
hard as stone, with a gold belt,
resembled the slopes of the Añjana mountain
encircled by a fresh ribbon of minerals.

adhārayad darśitadehasauṣṭavāṃ
sa rājasūnus tanuvṛttamadhyatām /
parākramatrāsitacittavṛttibhir
mṛgādhirājair upadīkṛtām iva // MV 3.9[110] //

This son of the king possessed
a slender circumference of the waist
enhancing the beauty of his body.
It was like a gift/bribe from the lions,
kings of the jungle,
with their hearts trembling because of his courage.

vyarājatoraḥsthalam asya tāvatā
viśālabhāvena kavāṭabandhuram /
karīndrakumbhapratimaṃ mṛgīdṛśāṃ
kucadvayaṃ yāti na yāvatā bahiḥ // MV 3.10 //

[110] The verse is given in accordance with reading proposed by Subrahmaṇya-śāstrī.

His charming panel-like chest shone.
(Even) the pair of women's breasts
similar to the globes on an elephant's head
does not cross such breadth.

ghanāṃsapīṭhau kaṭhināruṇāṅgulī
paṭuprakoṣṭhau parighānukārinau /
mahaujasas tasya manoharau bhujāv
apaśyad ājānuvilambinau janaḥ // MV 3.11 //

People noticed
his iron bar-like mighty and attractive arms,
with solid shoulder-blades and hard, reddish fingers,
strong fore-arms, hanging up to his knees.

vihāya madhyaṃ yadi lakṣmarekhayā
bahiḥ prasāryeta sudhāṃśumaṇḍalam /
daroditaśmaśrukṛtaśriyas tadā
tadānanendor upamānatāṃ vrajet // MV 3.12 //

If the series of spots could be removed
from the centre to the edge of its orb,
then the moon might attained resemblance
to his moon-like face made beautiful by the beard just visible.

vinidrapaṅkeruhadāla[em.; *ma* Ed.[111]]*dīrghayor*
dṛśor upānte janito 'sya śoṇimā /

[111] The word '*dāman*' means 'a gift, share, string, garland, large bandage', etc. (Monier-Williams 2005: 474–475). If we think about the conventional images obligatory in Sanskrit poetry, the emendation appears necessary: the shape of the eye is compared to the lotus petals. The word for petal in Sanskrit is however 'dala', not 'dāla'. According to the Monier Williams Dictionary: *dāla* means 'a kind of honey produced from petals'. However, we can understand *dāla* as 'belonging to petal, having its characteristics'. So Kampana's eyes are depicted as 'having the largeness typical for a lotus petal'. This particular stanza, similarly to all the verses of the third canto, is written in the *vaṃśastha* metre, which pattern (v—v—— v v—v—v —) requires a long syllable in that place; hence the choice of the poetess was most probably 'dāla'.

anargalasvaprasaraprarodhaka—
śrutidvayīdarśitaroṣayir iva // MV 3.13 //

In the corners of his eyes,
long like the petals of a blown lotus,
redness appeared,
as if showing anger towards the ears
that limited their freedom in expanding.

anulbaṇām āyatatuṅgabandhurām
amaṃsta lokaḥ sphuṭam asya nāsikām /
viśṛṅkhalavyāpnuvadīkṣaṇadvayī—
parasparākrāntinivāraṇārgalām // MV 3.14 //

People thought of his long,
prominent and slightly hooked nose
as a bar extended in order to prevent (his) eyes
from stepping upon each other's territory.

adhārayad garbhitaraktasandhyakaṃ
nṛpātmajaḥ keśakalāpam āyatam /
dṛḍhānurāgacchuritair mṛgīdṛśām
anupraviṣṭaṃ hṛdayair ivāntarā // MV 3.15 //

The prince had a mass of long hair
interlaced with red water-lily flowers,
as if inlaid with hearts of doe-eyed beauties
bound by the fetters of their passion (for him).

saha pratāpena samunnatiṃ vapur
valakṣa[em.: *valarkṣa* Ed.]*bhāvaṃ yaśasā vilocane* /
guṇaiḥ parīṇāham amuṣya kandharā
svareṇā gāmbhīryam agacchad āśayaḥ // MV 3.16 //

His body and strength grew,
his eyes and fame became white,
his neck along with his qualities widened,
his mind together with his voice became deeper.

Figure 5: Ideal man and woman. The pillar in Lepakshi Temple, Andhra Pradesh. (Photo L. Sudyka)

Figure 6: Figure of ideal woman (*padminī* type). The pillar in Lepakshi Temple, Andhra Pradesh. (Photo L. Sudyka)

Figure 7: Figure of ideal man. The pillar in Lepakshi Temple, Andhra Pradesh. (Photo L. Sudyka)

Figure 8: Face of ideal man. The pillar in Lepakshi Temple, Andhra Pradesh. (Photo L. Sudyka)

Such a depiction of a person from the bottom up, called *nakhaśikhāvarṇana*, belongs to the *kāvya* convention. Not surprisingly, a detailed description of a human body appears in the *Kāmasūtra* and other manuals on *ars amatoria* as well. Also *Manusmṛti*, *Yājñavalkyasmṛti*, *Viṣṇudharmasūtra* and *purāṇas* name qualities and faults of different parts of the body. This time the detailed information is important for predicting future or arranging a marriage. And of course *kāvya* descriptions of a beautiful woman and a handsome man make use of this culturally established repertoire.[112] In fact, Gaṅgādevī mentioned all good signs to be seen on the body of a newly born prince which clearly indicated his potential to become a good ruler. The second description shows the fully developed and mature prince. This time the poetess concentrates on the physical charms and attractiveness of his body described from tip to toe. Usually such *nakhaśikhāvarṇanas* concern the depiction of female beauty. However, the woman-writer is visibly more interested in presenting the body of her hero. There are no detailed descriptions of a woman's body in her poem at all. The only exception is the pregnant Bukka's queen.

On the other hand, male-writers prefer the *nakhaśikhāvarṇana* of a beauty and their presentation of a hero's body is usually limited to mentions about broad chest, strong arms long up to the

[112] According to the *Manusmṛti* (1.3.10), the good signs for a girl are a gait like a goose (*haṃsa*) or an elephant, a delicate body, not too hairy, and long hair. Other texts add small teeth, a neck like a sea-shell with three lines and a delicate body, etc. According to the *Garuḍa-Purāṇa* (1.63–65), a man should have arms round like the trunk of an elephant; a deep navel, voice and intellect; a broad forehead, chest and face, a long nose, arms, eyes, teeth and face; a tall neck (the three lines on it are also recommended), etc. Some of these traits are easy to spot while looking at the column from the Lepakshi temple interior (Anantapur District of Andhra Pradesh) presenting an ideal man (Fig. 7, 8) and woman (Fig. 6) of the physically superior type, i.e. *padminī*. The temple was developed during the 14th and 16th centuries and was an important pilgrimage centre in the Vijayanagara Empire. The paintings which are preserved in the *raṅga maṇḍapa* must represent faithfully the clothes and other details of everyday life at that time.

knee, the lion-like (i.e. thin) waist and the comparison of different parts of the body (face, eyes and limbs) to the lotus occurs.[113] Gaṅgādevī's description is full of erotic sentiment (*śṛṅgāra-rasa*) and the picture of Kampana nearly as an embodiment of Kāma is suggested. The 'local trait' enters the scene when Gaṅgā compares his buttocks to the slopes of Añjana,[114] a mountain so important in geographical and mythological landscape of the Vijayanagara city.

On attaining youth, the prince married several princesses, and this piece of information may have been accompanied also by the name/names of his principal consort or consorts, but the manuscript is damaged in this place and after the usual sequences of comparisons equalling the queens with the consorts of gods, there are lacunae in the text. Was our poetess among them? There is no other evidence than her own words contained in stanza MV 7.39 quoted earlier. The poetess speaks of herself as the king's beloved—*priyā*—but we cannot be sure of her status at the court. As far as we know, the literary circles were male-dominated and the only women that might easily participate in such communities were well-educated courtesans. On the other hand, it cannot be excluded that the princess whom Kampana married was educated and talented, as Gaṅgā's poem clearly shows.

Kampana as a husband and lover is shown in several cantos: 5, 6 and 7. The eroticism of the king and his harem was an important subject in *kāvya* literature. As David Smith notices in his recently published article "One man and many women: some notes on the harem in mainly ancient and medieval India from sundry perspectives":

---

[113] In devotional poems, no matter if composed by male or female writers, the god's, i.e. male, body is described in detail, but this time in the reverse order, from bottom to toe.

[114] Añjanādri—a place where Hanumān was born. The Hampi area was identified to be Kiṣkindhā, a monkey kingdom mentioned in the *Rāmāyaṇa*.

> At the centre of the production of Sanskrit poetry was the royal court; and at the centre of the court was the harem, the *antaḥpura*, *avarodhana*, *śuddhānta*. At first glance we might say that the centre of the court was the king on his throne. His harem came into the throne room with him, and flanking him from behind, as described in the *Mānasollāsa* (3.1161ff.). But rather than this public place, the centre, the secret heart of the palace was indeed the harem, where the king was more or less alone with his women.
> (...) the king was a great lover, or at least sought to be so seen. Such was the assertion of many medieval Sanskrit inscriptions, as well set out by Thomas Donaldson in his *Kamadeva's Pleasure Garden, Orissa*. Indian poetry and painting generally was fascinated by the erotic splendour of the king and his many wives.
> (Smith 2012: 4)

Kampana is shown with his women, too. We see his erotic prowess at the background of kaleidoscopic changes of seasons. All the descriptions are written in perfect accordance with the *kāvya* convention. This 'song' of seasons starts with the depiction of summer in 9 elegant strophes, afterwards monsoon time comes—14 stanzas presenting the fauna and flora during the rainy season, then the king in his harem. The standard, yet delightful depiction of autumn is contained in 13 verses. Also winter, the season usually neglected by *kāvya* writers, is presented in a longish passage (MV 5.51–61). In fact, here the poetess concentrates entirely on the king's lovemaking in wintertime and frankly declares this in the first couplet of this eleven-stanza-long description:

atha nṛpasya samutsukacetaso
madanakelikalāsu vilāsinaḥ /
priyam ivācaritum̩ samupāgamat
praguṇayan kṣaṇadās tuhināgamaḥ // MV 5.51 //

Then the winter came lengthening the nights,
as if to please the passionate king,
who longed for lovemaking.

Then the king and his womenfolk are shown in the inner apartments scented with *agaru* fumes (*ramaṇījanair agarugāndhiṣu garbhagṛheṣu*—MV 5.55cd), with beds strewn with fresh leaves of clove trees (*navalavaṅgataruprasavāstṛtāni śayitāni*—MV 5.57cd), engaged in lovemaking.

The next 14 stanzas, full of conventional images, offer a nice example of spring description. Canto 6, though not complete (*śloka*s 14–56 are missing), seems to be devoted to the water-sports of the king exclusively. Canto 7 depicts the sunset and night, again in a manner doing full justice to the *kāvya* tradition. There is, however, an unexpected personal touch in these standard descriptions: as we already know, Kampana, after performing his evening rituals or *sandhyāvandana*, addresses his favourite Gaṅgā, who is the authoress of the poem, to describe the beginning of night in elegant verses. Asked courteously by the king, she presents before him the description of the darkness and the moon, suitably to the subject addressing him as 'the moon among the kings' (*nṛpacandra*).

The comparison of Kampana to the god of love, Kāma, is a recurring motif in these passages. Take for instance the strophe showing the king's courting in wintertime:

iti sukhāny ucitāni himāgame
samanubhūya manobhavasannibhaḥ /
śiśirayāmavatīṣv api rāgavān
ramayituṃ ramaṇīr udayuṅkta saḥ // MV 5.56 //

> The impassioned king, who resembled the God of Love,
> stimulated his lovers to lovemaking,
> even if the nights were cold,
> thus enjoying the delights of winter.

Kampana is introduced as a good husband and a lover full of sexual energy and desire, enjoying the company of his women. The mention about newly married, inexperienced wives (MV 5.59d—*mugdhavadhujanaḥ*) underlines that his harem grew bigger and bigger.

Gaṅgādevī depicts Kampana as a good ruler. One could say that Kampana did not only listen to the words of his father but was following his wise advice provided in the excerpt finishing canto 3 (verses 21 to 43). King Bukka warns him off different sins of youth and addictions which can be dangerous especially for a king. Among these vices he mentions gambling, drinking, hunting and women, which in Kauṭilya's *Arthaśāstra* are classified as 'a fourfold group arising from desire' (*kāmajaś caturvarga*/ AŚ 8.3/ Jolly & Schmidt 1923:167). As mentioned above, Kampana's relationships with women suited the pattern[115] accepted for an Indian ruler. The other two vices, namely gambling and drinking, are not even mentioned in Gaṅgā's poem. In the *mahākāvya* tradition wine drinking usually is referred to when the night is being described. Canto 7 contains a depiction of the night, but the poetess, in elegant verses, presents mainly her observation on natural phenomena: the setting sun, the evening sky, the rising moon, lotuses, birds, stars, etc. In the picture of this evening hour, she introduces only women proceeding to a tryst or *abhisārikā*s (MV 7.31). Then, as we know, two actors appear on the scene: Kampana and Gaṅgā, and a short conversation takes place culminating in *ex tempore* creation of a short 'nocturnal' poem finishing the canto.

As to hunting, Bukka warns his son:

vinā phalaṃ jīvitasaṃśayapradāṃ
vinodabuddhyā mṛgayāṃ bhajeta kaḥ /
pramādyatāṃ pārthivagandhahastināṃ
iyaṃ hi vārī kathitā vicakṣaṇaiḥ // MV 3.29 //

> Who will indulge in hunting endangering his own life
> without any gain, only with the intention to diverse himself?

115 "From the *Rāmāyaṇa* onward, the analogy of the king and his wives is that of the bull and his cows, and the bull elephant and his cow elephants. The royal court with its dozens or hundreds of sexual partners for the king alone is consciously and specifically modelled on the single bull with his herd of cows, or a bull elephant with female elephants. The bull-like king ipso facto has superior sexual powers" (Smith 2012: 2).

Wise men used to call it a trap for
passionate kings as well elephants in rut.

It is stated in the *Arthaśāstra* that if we were to choose between hunting and gambling, hunting is the worse vice of the human race, since falling into the hands of robbers and enemies, getting into wildfire, fear, inability to distinguish between the cardinal points, hunger, thirst and loss of life are evils consequent upon it. But there are also positive things which should be said about hunting, remarks Kauṭilya. It provides a good exercise causing the disappearance of phlegm, bile, fat and sweat. Additionally, it gives a chance to develop different skills, such as, for instance, aiming at stationary and moving bodies (AŚ 8.3). Hunting was considered not only a favourite pastime and sport of Indian kings but almost their duty. As Rājā Rudradeva (c. 15–16th century) explains in his *Śyainika Śāstra* or the "Book on Hawking", royal hunting leads to the acquisition of merits by killing ferocious animals, such as wolves and tigers. By the slaughter of stags and other animals, crop is protected (*vadhena hariṇādīnāṃ śasyādīnañ ca rakṣaṇāt*—ŚŚ 3.22cd). It is also a good occasion for an inspection of the forest, which again can serve many useful purposes, such as frightening thieves and conciliating forest tribes (ŚŚ 3.23). Defined as such, hunting belongs to the *rājadharma* or king's code of conduct, one can say.

Kampana, engaging himself in hunting, proves to follow the path of a righteous sovereign fulfilling one of his duties:

hatatarakṣu parikṣatasairibhaṃ
mṛditaraṅku niṣūditasūkaram /
glapitakhaḍgī gṛhītamataṅgajaṃ
vanam asau mṛgayāsu muhur vyadhāt // MV 5.14 //

During his hunting expeditions,
he constantly cleared the forest,
slaughtering hyenas, killing buffaloes and deer,

exterminating wild boars, subduing rhinos
and catching wild elephants.

It is clearly visible that the purpose of his hunting escapades was not the self-enjoyment but protecting his subjects from wild and dangerous animals. Kampana and his men did catch the elephants, as they could be tamed and used, and their killing was even prohibited, if not in battle. The hunting expeditions of Kampana took place after defeating Sambhuvarāya, when Kampana was staying in Kāñcīpuram.

At that time his subjects benefited also from his intelligence and novel methods of management, which he brought to perfection (MV 5.3b—*abhuṅkta navām nayasaṃpadām*). What new methods are alluded to here? Perhaps the organization of the administrative system characteristic of the Vijayanagara Empire is mentioned here. As K.A. Nilakanta Sastri points out, Harihara I shaped the administrative system following the model of the Kākatīyas (Nilakanta Sastri 1958: 254). He appointed the so-called *karṇikas* over 3–5 hamlets, *sthalakaraṇas* over 20–30 villages and *nāḍu-gauḍas* and *nāḍu-talaiyārs* over the region (Venkataramanayya 1942: 187). As Burton Stein states:

> Administrative specialists provided a web upon which the entire fabric of Vijayanagara politics was intricately woven.
> (Stein 1997: 91)

According to K.G. Krishnan, the first administrative step connected with the effective management of the newly annexed area:

> (...) was to arrange for the formation of convenient territorial divisions which can be easily governed. They were designed as *rājyas* in consistence with the vastness of the empire transcending the usual devisions of *kōṭṭam or vaḷanāḍu, nāḍu* etc., which were current in the previous regional regimes (...). The area under Tamil Nadu was organised as five *rājyas*—Chandragiri-rājyam, Paḍaivīḍu-rājyam, Tiruvadigai-rājyam, Chōḷa-rājyam and Madurai or Pāṇḍya-rājyam. (...) Many readjustments were made some-

> times by changing the name as in the case of Rājagambhīra into Paḍaivīḍu-rājya (...).
> (Krishnan 2006: 16)

Interestingly enough, the name of Rājagambhīra was changed as if to cover the past of this territory. Perhaps the name of Rājagambhīra was too strongly connected with the Sambhuvarāyas. After all, it was the name of the ancestor of Camparāya, Rājagambhīra, a subordinte od Rājarāja III. It should be noticed here that *paḍaivīḍu* means 'encampment', and according to stanza MV 4.67,[116] the town at the foot of the hill was transformed into the camp of the Vijanagara army besieging the fortress of Rājagambhīra and possibly the new name (today Padavedu) commemorates this fact.

In the early Vijayanagara inscriptions coming from Tamil Nadu, titles such as *mahāmaṇḍaleśvara* and *mahāpradhāni* appear. People bearing such titles must have been administrators, provincial governors supervising the work of their subordinates *adhikāri*s and building the whole bureaucratic machine enabling the Vijayanagara ruler to govern the territory through his officers. Velcheru Narayana Rao, David Shulman and Sanjay Subrahmanyam stress in their book that the main impact of Kampana's campaign consisted in:

> (...) settlement of Telugu and Kannadiga warrior lineages in the Tamil country to a far greater extent than had ever been experienced before. Conspicuous figures such as Gaṇḍāraguḷi Mārayya Nāyaka (a warrior-leader of major significance in the South Arcot region in the third quarter of the fourteenth century), should be seen not merely as the 'agents' of Kampana's will, but as semi-autonomous actors, whose significance for rural political economy was far longer-lasting than the Vijayanagara campaigns orchestrated by Kampana.
> (Rao, Shulman & Subrahmanyam 1992: 29)

[116] For the text and translation of this stanza see: p. 81.

The *nāyaṃkara* and *ayagar* systems[117] will develop in the next stage only.

Kampana introduced a system of light taxation in his dominion (MV 5.5ab—*karaparigraham (...) mṛdutaram*). He also used the methods recommended to a king by the *Arthaśāstra*, namely "nothing could be unnoticed in provinces of friends and foes alike by him, who was employing many spies" (MV 5.4 abc: *asuhṛdāṃ suhṛdāṃ iva maṇḍaleṣu ajani tena na kiñcid alakṣitam prahitacāragaṇena*). He granted audience to crowds of kings of different countries named duly in stanza 5.9. On his both sides the beautiful ladies waved the chowris, and in the jingling of their golden bracelets, the voice of court bards—*māgadhas*, singing panegyrics—*birudāvalis*, was almost drowned (MV 5.10[118]). It seems that *biruda gadya* recitation was part and parcel of everyday life at the royal courts in South India. In the morning, the royal *vāndins or māgadhas* recited these eulogies to the king. Nilakanta Sastri calls *biruda gadya* "a type of historical composition standing midway between the *praśastis* in the inscriptions and the chronicles"(Nilakanta Sastri 1964: 86). *Biruda gadyas* preserved and transmitted by the *bhat* community grew in contents and

---

[117] *Nāyaṃkara*—a form of military land tenure. This Vijayanagara system originated most probably "as an Indic adaptation of the Islamicate system of administration through *iqtā*[c] assignements. As formulated under the Saljuqs, the *iqtā*[c] was an assignement of the right to collect land revenue, in return for which the *iqtā*[c]—holder was obliged to provide military service for the state". (Wagoner 2000: 318) *Ayagar*—a paid village servants system.

[118] *parisaradvayacāmaradhāriṇī-*
kanakakaṅkaṇariṅkhaṇanisvanaḥ /
aśamayan nṛpater birudāvalī-
mukharamāgadhamaṇḍalavaikharīm // MV 5.10//

The sound of moving gold bracelets of
the women waving chowris on both sides
deadened the voice of a group of bards
singing panegyrics to the king.

length during the oral transmission, resulting finally, after a few generations, in a new shape, that of a chronicle. Unfortunately only few of these have survived.[119]

Kampana's glory was sung not only by the bards. The ladies of the court used to play different musical instruments to accompany songs telling of his acts of glory (MV 5.12). The remaining *śloka*s of this 76-stanza-long chapter, as already mentioned, depict the king and his beloveds' entertainments in the setting of different seasons of the year.

The three chapters, though purely descriptive and full of conventional images, possibly provide us with information of historical value. Perhaps these chapters can be treated as a testimony that Kampana's rule in the Tamil country was well established and really welcomed by the inhabitants of Tuṇḍīramaṇḍala. That is why the ruler, feeling safe, could devote so much time to diverse entertainments, not without forgetting about affairs of state (MV 6.69).

This happy and peaceful life in Kāñcīpuram[120] lasted several years. Those were the years when information concerning the situation in the neighbouring Madurai Sultanate[121] was gathered.

---

[119] The most famous among them is the *Rāmrājīyam*, telling the history of the Aravidu dynasty.

[120] In the MV, besides the mention that Kāñcīpuram was a big city "which was like an ornament to this earth" (MV 5.1), there is no description of the city proper: perhaps Gaṅgādevī, after supplying the reader with the description of The City of Victory standing for the symbol of the empire, considered another description of the town superfluous. It is also possible that Kampana and his court after some time moved to Mulbāgal, the capital of his viceroyalty.

[121] The Madurai Sultanate was a short-lived result of Muslim expansion to the South. In 1311 Malik Kāfūr led the army of the Deccan Sultanates against the Pāṇḍya kingdom and sacked Madurai. The other two Muslim expeditions were in 1314 and 1323, when Muslims managed to establish a viceroyalty for the Delhi Sultanate in Madurai. In 1333 Jalāl ud-Dīn Ahsan Shāh became an independent ruler of Madurai. He was succeeded by Alā ud-Dīn Udaiji (1339–1340), Qutb ud-Dīn (1340), Ghiyās ud-Dīn Damghani (1341–1343), Nasiruddin (1343–1352) and Qurbat Hasan Kangu (1353–1370).

Figure 9: Cidambaram Temple. (Photo A. Nitecka)

Figure 10: Śrīraṅgam Temple. (Photo L. Sudyka)

Figure 11: Madurai Temple. (Photo J. Sudyka)

The campaign against Madurai was carried on between 1365 and 1370[122] (Nilkanta Sastri 1958: 256; Stein 1997: 28). The rule of Qurbat Hasan Kangu, who had been brought from Daulatabad to fill the vacant throne in Madurai, was disastrous. He knew too little about the political situation; additionally, his character and behaviour disappointed his own people, which is corroborated by Shams Siraj Afif's *Tārīkh-i-Fīrūz-Shāhī* (Thiruvenkatachari 1957: 52). It was a really good moment for Vijayanagara to launch an attack in order to extend the kingdom and expel the enemies. At that moment Kampana, playing the part of Rāma, could wage a war against Turuṣka, who behaved like Rāvaṇa, as his father Bukka I stated (MV 3.43). For Kampana it was a favourable opportunity to acquire widespread fame and strengthen the Vijayanagara position immensely. The scions of old southern dynasties—Vīra Pāṇḍya, Sundara Pāṇḍya Rāmadeva and Vīra Ballāla III—submitted, lost their lives or ran away from Muslim power. According to Vijayanagara dynastic legends[123] recorded in later sources, sage Vidyāraṇya asked the Sangama brothers, who were at that time in the service of Mohammedan governor, to rescue Śiva and other gods from Muslims, and his request became their sacred *dharmic* mission.

What does Gaṅgādevī say about the direct reasons for the struggle undertaken against Muslims?

[122] Even before 1365, Sāvaṇṇa, the governor of Kampana, started preparing the ground for his cousin, subduing some territories as far as those in the Tanjavur District. The proof confirming a stable situation in the country after defeating the Muslims is offered by the fact that in 1371 the image of Raṅganātha was brought back, as the inscription in the Raṅganātha temple in Śrīraṅgam says.

[123] Different versions connected with the beginnings of the Vijayanagara city and kingdom are related in the *Vidyāraṇyavṛttānta, Vidyāraṇyakālajñāna, Rājakālanirṇaya, Guruvaṃśa*, Tamil, Kannada and Telugu chronicles and accounts of foreign travellers and Muslim historians. The first three historiographic narratives were discussed in detail and confronted with Muslim sources in the article "Harihara, Bukka and the Sultan. The Delhi Sultanate in the Political Imagination of Vijayanagara" by Philip Wagoner.

Unfortunately, sarga 8 lacks the first *ślokas*. The remaining stanzas describe the poor condition of the Tamil country under Muslim occupation. Three places extremely important for every Hindu are mentioned: Cidambaram (Fig. 9), Śrīraṅgam (Fig. 10) and Madhurā (present Madurai—Fig. 11). The poetess puns on another name of Cidambaram, namely Vyāghrapuri.[124] She says that it has now become a real city of tigers. The desolated Śrīraṅga temple complex is guarded only by the lord of serpents. In the ruined temples one can hear the howl of jackals instead of the sound of temple drums (*mṛdaṅga*). The doors are worm-eaten and grass is growing in the temple halls (*maṇḍapa*). The inner shrines (*garbhagṛha*) are in ruins. The Tāmraparṇī's waters are red with the blood of slaughtered cows. The Kāverī has forgotten its boundaries and causes destruction.[125] In the Brahmanas' settlements (*agrahāras*), the smoke of sacrifices and the sound of Veda chanting has been replaced by the smell of meat and voices of drunken Turuṣkas. Coconut groves in Madhurā do not exist. There are rows of iron spikes with heads on them. In the streets of Madhurā, instead of the charming sounds of women's anklets, the noise produced by the chains of Brahmanas is heard. In the houses of Yavanas, parrots are taught to speak Persian.[126]

---

[124] This name can be connected with the legend recorded in the *Cidambaramāhātmya*, which concerns the mythical sage Vyāghrapāda, who came to the holy lake of Cidambaram and worshipped the liṅga at Śivagaṅgā. Then god Śiva arrived there and for the first time performed his cosmic dance.

[125] It is highly probable that the lack of routine irrigation works caused floods.

[126] *na tathā kaṭughūtkṛtāt vyathā me*
hṛdi jīrṇopavaneṣu ghūkalokāt /
pariśīlitapārasīkavāgbhyo
yavanānāṃ bhavane yathā śukebhyaḥ // MV 8.12 //

"It is not the harsh hoots
of owl broods
in gardens run wild,
so much as the parrots practising Persian

In the *kāvya* tradition the description of the city creates the feeling of amazement and admiration, also for the king who lives in such a beautiful capital. Here the description is the cause of utmost fear and disgust. We face the negation of the usual role of the description of the city. A literary parallel for this picture can be found in Kālidāsa's *Raghuvaṃśa, sarga* 16.[127] What is the historical truth hidden behind this literary device?

Persian historians and poets, such as Amīr Khusrau (*Tārikh-ī-Alai*) and Ziyā' al-Dīn Baranī (*Tārīkh-i Fīrūz Shāhī*), also the accounts of Ibn Batuta, Firishta, to name but a few (Hodivala 1957: 102–103), but mainly South Indian inscriptions and *sthala-purāṇas* of Śrīraṅgam, Madhurā and Kāñcīpuram, and other literary sources provide us with equally frightful details of Muslim policy towards Hindus. Thus the description contained in the *Madhurāvijaya* appears to concur with other sources as far the poor condition of the Tamil country under Muslim occupation is considered.

Malik Kāfūr's raid in 1311 left Madhurā temples plundered (Nelson 1989 3.2: 81–82), and the Pāṇḍya king abandoned his capital. According to the temple's chronicle, festival images of the deities had been carried to Kerala safely. The Mīnākṣi Temple priests ran away. Before leaving, they managed to seal *sanctum sanctorum* of Sundareśvara and place a substitute *liṅga* in front of it. The invaders pulled down the outer walls of the temple, ruined many buildings and soon only the shrines of Mīnākṣi and Sundareśvara were left intact.[128]

---

in the dwellings of the foreign princelings
that torments me."

(Rajaraman & Kotamraju 2013: 97)

[127] See the forthcoming article "Women Town—Ghost Town" by Tomasz Winiarski, in Cracow Indological Studies, vol. 15, 2013.

[128] As legend has it, when Kampana entered the Mīnākṣi Temple after defeating the Muslims, a Kulaśekhara Perumān opened the sealed *sanctum sancto-*

In Śrīraṅgam thousands of Vaiṣṇavas lost their lives. It is related that the main shrine was walled up in order to protect *garbhagṛha* and its Sleeping Beauty *mūlabimbam* from the invaders whereas the *utsavabimbam*[129]—Smiling Beauty—was taken to the north and given shelter in Tirupati. The manuscripts of *Śrutaprakāśikā*, the commentary on the *Śrībhaṣya*, were entrusted to Śrī Vedanta Deśika, who found shelter in a remote village. It is believed that at that time he composed *Abhītistavam*—*Hymn of Fearlessness*—containing 29 stanzas which prayed for being rid of fear and the enemies of Lord Raṅganātha and his devotees. In several stanzas he asks the Lord to destroy the fear that seized those in Śrīraṅgam (*bhayam śamatha raṅgadhāmni*—stanza 20), to establish once again the sway of *dharma* in Śrīraṅgam, his great abode (*punaḥ pravartayatu dhāmni te mahati dharmacakrasthitim*—stanza 23 b) and to allay the fear in Śrīraṅgam and other *kṣetras* caused by the foes who are like cruel demons (*danuprabhavadāruṇa*).[130] In stanza 22 he enumerates these foes and the creators of fear at the same time. He prays:

kalipraṇidhilakṣaṇaiḥ kalitaśākyalokāyataiḥ
turuṣkayavanādibhir jagati jṛmbhamāṇaṃ bhayam /

---

rum and it turned out that the lamp left almost seventy years previously was still burning and sandal paste and flowers were fresh. Kulaśekhara Perumān, due to the fact that the miracle had taken place in his presence, was appointed chief priest (*sthānika*) by Kampana. After a few years, Kampana, dissatisfied with his and his family conduct, decided that Sadāśiva was worthy of that position. The decision caused a conflict between Kulaśekharas and Vikkira Pantiyas (Fuller 2007: 32–33).

[129] The deity taken out in procession is known as the *utsavar*, *utsavabimbam*, *utsavamūrti* or *kautukabimbam*. The main deity remaining in the shrine is called *moolavar*, *mūlabimbam*.

[130] *manuprabhṛtimānite mahati raṅgadhāmādike*
danuprabhavadāruṇair daram udīryamāṇaṃ paraḥ /
prakṛṣṭaguṇaka śriyā vasudhayā sandhukṣitaḥ
prayuktakaraṇodadhiḥ praśamaya svaśaktyā svayam // AS 24 //

prakṛṣṭanijaśaktibhiḥ prasabham āyudhaiḥ pañcabhiḥ
kṣititridaśarakṣakaiḥ kṣapaya raṅganātha kṣaṇāt // AS 22 //

O Raṅganātha, with Thy five weapons,
known as extremely powerful
and protecting gods of the earth (i.e. Brahmanas),
destroy in a trice the fear growing in the world,
caused by the emissaries of the Kaliyuga:
Buddhists, Lokāyatas, Turuṣkas, Yavanas and others.

Also the *Madhurāvijaya* underlines the links of the Muslims with the Kali age:

udagram agre yavanādhibhartuḥ
sākṣāt kaler maulim ivāśugena /
sa maṅkṣu sārdhaṃ jayakāṅkṣitena
dhvāṅkṣadhvajaṃ dhvaṃsayati sma dhanvī // MV 9.32 //

First, this bowman (Kampana) quickly destroyed,
with an arrow longing for victory,
the projecting crow banner of the Yavana king,
evidently resembling the crest of the Kali age.

A Vilasa Grant of Prolaya Nayaka (issued between 1325 and 1350 A.D.), discussed by Cynthia Talbot in detail in her article "Inscribing the Other, Inscribing the Self: Hindu-Muslim Identities in Pre-Colonial India"(Talbot 1995), lists all the atrocities and vileness of Muslim rule in Andhra after the death of the righteous king Pratāparudra Kākatīya: the desecration of the temples, the confiscation of Brahmana villages, the slaying the Brahmanas. Of course, bad Muslim habits such as drinking wine and eating beef are also mentioned. Cynthia Talbot notices that the stylistics of the Vilasa Grant is very close to a popular literary convention and reminds us the rhetoric and contents of the *purāṇas*:

> Among the contents of the major puranas is the history of India, narrated in the form of royal genealogies that end in the fourth century C.E. with the dynasties of the Kali age, the fourth and last

> era in the cycle of time. In the ancient Indian conception, truth and morality declined in each successive era, and one of the main symptoms of the Kali age's degeneracy was the growing strength of foreign dynasties. Because political power would increasingly pass into the hands of foreigners and non-royal Indians, the puranas prophesied a terrible future.
> (Talbot 1995: 697)

The *purāṇas*, the Vilasa Grant and the *Abhītistavam* definitely reflect the anxieties of their Brahmana composers and preservers of the Brahmanical culture at certain historical moment, their fear (*abhīti*) of barbarians who, like the demons, do not know and do not obey the rules of *dharma*. They were afraid to lose their position and privileges. Muslim attacks affected mainly the Brahmanas as they controlled the temples and the performance of rituals. They were also deprived of tax-exempt villages. The core of the Brahmanic world was endangered as it had happened in the past with the advance of Buddhism or encounters with Hunas, Śakas and Yavanas. All of them belonged to a different, unknown world and as such they were demonized. As Cynthia Talbot stresses, in the Vilasa Grant there are no allusions to Islamic and religious beliefs or doctrines and the word 'Muslim' does not appear at all. The Muslim invaders were called Turks, Persians or even Greeks, a fact which confirms that the sense of difference between 'us' and 'them' was not primarily grounded on a religious base. They were considered one more ethnic community in India among many others.

Cynthia Talbot's words concerning Prolaya Nayaka chief, hailing from the Musunuri family of the Kamma caste, turn out to be applicable to the Sangama rulers as well. They were also warriors of a low social position and, after establishing their realm, in their quest for acceptance as legitimate kings, they also sought the most prestigious support possible, namely 'the use of the all-India literary language of Sanskrit, the patronage of Brahmins' (Talbot 1995: 703). They also included the memory of previous dynasties into their cleverly created image.

What should also be stressed, in the medieval history of India, temple desecrations were recorded in connection with conflicts between Hindu rulers, too. In 642 A.D. Narasiṃhavarman I looted an image of Gaṇeśa from the capital of the Cālukyas. Rajendra Cola I brought to his capital several images seized from neighbouring kings (Eaton 2000: 256). One could multiply the examples of stealing or destroying the images of *rāṣṭra-devatās*, which were the symbol of dynastic power. Temples were institutions of great political significance. The cases of temple desecrations by Muslims received special attention from certain historians[131] (Eaton 2000: 246–247), a fact which obviously resulted in the creation of communalistic atmosphere, although they belonged to the pattern observed in the medieval period of the history of India on both Hindu and Muslim sides.

If we come back to the *Madhurāvijaya* and its literary form, we can see that the affiliation to the court epic poem genre (*mahākāvya, sargabandha*) offers the symbolism of the fight against demons undertaken in order to save the world.[132]

[131] Some of these historians, such as Sir Henry M. Elliot, were keen to contrast the British enlightened rule with the cruelty and despotism of the Muhammadan invaders. The fact that this was a very successful policy becomes obvious while reading the Introduction to the second edition of the *Madhurāvijaya*, in which T. A. Gopinatha Rao commented on the end of the Vijayanagara Empire in such words: "The barrier in the shape of the Empire of Vijayanagara, which was raised by the hand of Providence to protect the virgin south from that ravishment her sister Northern India had suffered at the merciless and vandalistic hands of the Muhammadans, continued in fact for over two centuries until the fateful year A.D. 1565, when the magnificent Empire was shattered at the battle-field of Talikota by the confederacy of the Sultans of Bijapur, Golconda, etc. and the south became once again a prey to anarchy and disorder. Providence, at this juncture, ushered on the stage the British nation, who have once again restored order and peace over the whole of India" (Sastri & Sastri 1924: 15).

[132] More about *mahākāvya* as described by theoreticians of Indian literature in Chapter 4.

3.5. The Goddess with a sword

The above-presented description of the Tamil country under Muslim rule opening canto 8 is offered by a mysterious woman who appears before Kampana. Finally, she presents Kampana with a sword, explaining that the sword was made by Viśvakarman for god Śiva. Śiva gave it to the Pāṇḍya kings once, but it is time to change the possessor of the divine weapon as "the Pāṇḍya race has lost its virility by the wearing influence of time" (*kālavaśena pāṇḍyavaṃśyān gatavīryān avadhārya* (...)—canto 8[133]). It was Sage Agastya,[134] the custodian of the culture of the South, who decided to give the sword to King Kampana. As Nilakanta Sastri points out:

> The meaning behind the poetic conception is clear. The failure of the Pāndyan kings to recover Madura is the historic justification for Kampana's conquest of the Madura country; moreover, in the Pāndyan kingdom, the task of the Vijayanagara rulers was the continuance of the work of the ancient rulers of the land.
> (Sastri 1972: 214)

The mysterious lady, after handing in the scimitar, once more reminds us of the awful appearance and behaviour of Turuṣkas and their women, and appeals to Kampana:

nihitāhitalohitāmbuvarṣair nṛpa
nirvāpaya tāpam urvarāyāḥ //

May you, king, by the rain of enemies' blood
allay the sufferings of the earth!

S. Thiruvenkatachari suggests that the lady may be taken as the personification of suffering Dharma, who will be reinstalled

133 In the editions of the *Madhurāvijaya*, the stanzas of chapter 8 and the final one are not numbered as there are some lacunae in the text.

134 Agastya also equipped Rāma with the weapon.

Figure 12: Bhramarāmbikā handing down a scimitar to Śivajī, Śriśailam, Mallikārjuna temple complex. (Photo L. Sudyka)

Figure 13: Royal crest of Vijayanagara rulers. Varadarāja temple, Kāñcīpuram. (Photo L. Sudyka)

now by the Vijayanagara king (Thiruvenkatachari 1957: 9–10). In this figure one could also see *Rājyalakṣmī* (Royal Fortune), who has left Pāṇḍyan kings and chosen Kampana as her husband. Julia Hamper Hiebert sees "a divine water nymph" in this unnamed female figure (Hiebert 1985: 99). Perhaps she connects the appearance of the woman just before the battle with mythological beings, namely *apsaras*es, the female spirits taking care of the heroes dying in battles. Panduranga Bhatta, in his book *Contribution of Karnāṭaka to Sanskrit*, states that "the guardian deity of the city of Marakaṭapura appears to Kaṃpana in a vision" (Bhatta 1997: 109).

In fact, due to the lacunae in the *Madhurāvijaya* manuscript and the absence of the first stanzas in the eighth canto, the only thing we know about the woman is that she acts as Agastya's messenger and the sword is a divine weapon; the facts make us think that the woman herself is also a divine being.

The goddess offering a sword to the king appears in the Telugu "dynastic chronicle" of the early 16th century, Ekāmranātha's *Pratāparudracaritramu*. The legendary founder of the Kākatīya dynasty, Mādhava Varman, receives a divine sword and shield from goddess Padmākṣi to rule successfully with their help and transfer both talismans to his successors, who "will occupy the throne for one thousand years".[135] Also the famous Maratha ruler, Śivajī, was equipped with an invincible weapon by the goddess. In fact, two places aspire to be the scene of this event: Tuljapur in Maharashtra and Śriśailam in Andhra. In the Tuljapur story, Bhavāni comes to Shivajī in his dream and leaves the token of her protection—the sword. As the Śriśailam legend has it, Śivajī, while meditating near the Mallikārjuna Temple,[136] was about to

[135] Wagoner 1993: 43.

[136] Among other rulers, the kings of Vijayanagara, starting from Harihara II, made donations to this temple of great religious, historical and architectural significance.

leave this world. He raised his sword to cut off his head before the goddess Bhramarāmbikā. At that moment the goddess appeared, prophesied victory and everlasting fame to him, and presented a scimitar to him (Fig. 12) for protection of Hindu *dharma*. Both goddesses are considered to be aspects of Pārvatī.

Such traits as obtaining a divine helper and subsequently magic objects are typical for orally transmitted folk narratives and the motif of a god empowering the first ruler is popular in dynastic legends. What is also worth stressing in the story as told by Gaṅgādevī is the fact that the sword is described as Śiva's gift to Pāṇḍyas. Śiva as a giver of divine weapons is well known from the Kairata episode, which in different versions spread wide in Karnataka and Tamil Nadu due to the Śaiva inclinations of the South Indian royal houses. Under the patronage of these rulers, the Kairata episode inspired many works of art, and it seems that the image of Arjuna, the great warrior-ascetic, to whom the gods spoke and gave weapons in order to make him invincible and secure his victory, was particularly attractive for the ambitious local rulers of the South aspiring to the identification with Great Tradition.

On the other hand, Cornelia Mallebrein and Heinrich von Stietencron in their book *The Divine Play on Earth. Religious Aesthetics and Ritual in Orissa*, while discussing the figure of a still active Zamindar Raja in Bhatapada Garh, inform that:

> For his ancestors the Raja keeps a special room for worship (*iśāna*), where he also keeps his weapons, including the royal sword or *pāṭkhaṇḍa*, containing the power (*śakti*) of his *iṣṭadevī* goddess Siddheśvari.
> (Mallebrein & Stietencron 2008: 49)

The connections between the Orissan rulers and their tutelary goddesses were very complex and involved even taking over the *iṣṭadevī* of the former dynasty (Mallebrein & Stietencron 2008: 45). Similarly, the goddess of Pāṇḍyas could be associated with the new power in the region.

In the early 16th century, most likely during Kṛṣṇadevarāya's reign, the *Sāmrājyalakṣmīpīṭhikā*, showing the links between Sāmrājyalakṣmī and a king, was composed. Due to certain tantric practices the goddess could help a ruler to acquire power and god-like status on earth.

And such a goddess connected with Pāṇḍyan rulers was the goddess Mināksi of Madurai, who is depicted as a great warrior. She could not defeat only Śiva, her future husband. It might be that the divine lady described in the *Madhurāvijaya* is Mināksi herself, empowering the hero to subdue Muhammadan invaders of Madurai. In fact, such an identification one can find in the booklet *The Great Temple of Madurai*, being an English version of *Kōyilmānakar* by K. Palaniappan. The author of the book collects legends connected with the Madurai temple and in the chapter "Some miracles of later days" there is a story "Kambannar is Given a Sword", in which we read:

> It is said that in a dream the Goddess Meenakshi appeared before him and gave him a sword saying "This was given to Siva by Visvakarma. Siva gave it to the Pandyans, but they have lost ability to use this sword. Agasthyar has asked me to give this sword to you. Take it and save the people of the Pandyan Kingdom from the Muslims".
> (This incident is mentioned in the Sanskrit work Madurai Vijayam, written by Kambannar's wife Ganga Devi).
> (Palaniappan 1970: 59)

Having taken all this into consideration, it seems only natural that, in order to make the biography of her king more interesting and to the taste of the audience, not forgetting the divine legitimation of the undertaken war and his rule in the Tamil country, Gaṅgādevī introduced such a motif into her narration. We do not know if she really aimed at depicting the goddess Mīnākṣi;[137] if

[137] There is one more 'trace' of Madurai and Mīnākṣi in Gaṅgā's work, namely after the usual formula finishing canto I, we read: *mīnākṣai namaḥ*.

so, it would be again a clever move to strengthen the position of Vijayanagara in Tamil Nadu. In case the mysterious woman represented some other personage or idea, the above quoted fragment, a kind of *post scriptum* to Gaṅgā's poem, is a proof of how it could have been interpreted by a Tamilian receiver of the story.

Perhaps it is also worth mentioning that the royal crest of Vijayanagara rulers has the figure of a sword which stands on its point by the side of a boar (Fig. 13). As N. Venkata Ramanayya suggests the kings of Vijayanagara are indebted for this crest to the Kākatīyas, who took the boar crest symbolizing the imperial power from the Cālukyas (Ramanyya 1933: 102–103). If it is so, it sheds light on the policy of the first Vijayanagara rulers. They aptly used the symbols of earlier dynasties: the boar and the sword of the Kākatīyas and the sacred site of the Hoysalas became their crest and capital respectively. In the Penugonda inscription, it is stressed that Bukka I ruled over the kingdom of the Hoysalas from Hosapaṭṭaṇa, which obviously suggests that in this way he introduced himself as a successor of Hoysala kings or even more universal ruler—Sultan among the Hindu kings—*hiṃḍurāyasuratrāṇa*.[138] Later on, during the expansion on the Tamil country, the story connecting them with the Pāṇḍyas was

[138] The Penugoṇḍa Inscription of Bukka I (On the wall of the bastion on the north gate of the fort) dated Saka 127, Jaya, Caitra su. 1, corresponding to 1354 A.D., March 25.

1. *namastuṃga-śiraś-cuṃbi-caṃdra-cāmara-cāravē / trailōkya-nagarārambha-mūlastaṃbhāya śaṃbhavē // svasti [*] śrī*
2. *jayābhyudaya śaka-varṣa 1276 neya jaya-saṃvacarada caitra śu [1] maṃ svasti [*] śrīman-mahāmaṃḍa*
3. *śvara arirāya-vibhāḍa bhāṣege tappuva rāyara gaṃḍa hiṃḍurāya-suratrāṇa pūrvva- paścima-samudrā-*
4. *dhipati śrī vīra-bukkaṃṇa-voḍeyaru hoïsaḷānvaya-mahīpālara mēdinī-maṃḍalavanu ni[ja]-bhujamaṃ-*
5. *ḍanavāgi pālisu[tha] hosapaṭṭaṇadali sukha-saṃkathā-vinōdadiṃ rājyaṃ geyyutta tanna paṭṭadarasi jo[mmā]dēvi-*

narrated in order to make them 'familiar' and in the 'right place' in the Tamil country. In this way the Sangama lineage could be seen as continuing the traditions of older royal families. Such a confirmation was necessary for them, as it was once needed for Kullotuṅga I. Hermann Kulke, in his article "Functional Interpretation of a South Indian Māhātmya: The Legend of Hiraṇyavarman and the Life of the Cōḻa King Kulottuṅga", shows how a transformed temple legend could strengthen Kulottuṅga's claim to the Cola throne. The story about the sage Vyāghrapāda is amended by the introduction of the person of the legendary king Hiraṇyavarman in the last section of the *māhātmya*. His story is full of allusions to a historical situation, and he himself becomes a kind of porte-parole of Kulottuṅga. The handing over of a tiger banner to Hiraṇyavarman by Vyāghrapāda is the culminating moment for the story, and it can be understood as the sanctification of Kulottuṅga's rule. The tiger flag is the royal symbol of the Colas and obviously it meant the adoption to the royal line. We have an interesting addition to the legend of Hiraṇyavarman, namely the story of 3000 Brahmanas whom Hiraṇyavarman brought to Cidambaram. Hermann Kulke suggests that Kulottuṅga settled the priests from his own country as the story about their settlement becomes part of Cidambaram's sanctity after the 12th century. "As newcomers, these newly settled priests might have faced the problems similar to those of King Kulottuṅga" (Kulke 2001a: 203). That is why the story about the legendary king and a group of priests, with Lord Śiva as one of them, appears and gets its place

6. *yara kumāra śrī vīra-virupaṃṇa-voḍeyarige penugoṃ[ḍeya] rā[jyava]nu koṭṭu ā paṭṭaṇadalu sukhadiṃ*

7. *rājyava pālisutta penugoṃḍege sthaḷadurggavāgi mahāprathāna ananta[ra]sa-voḍeyaru māḍisida [sī]ḷida kalla kō-*

8. *[ṭe] dōni gottaḷavaṃka baḍagaṇa saṃtheya hebbāgelige maṃgaḷamahā śrī śrī śrī*

(Gopal & Ritti 2004: 53–54).

in the *Cidambaramāhātmya*, still experiencing some changes after the death of Kulottuṅga, and finally becomes a part of collective memory.

As one may notice something similar happened in the case of the Vijayanagara Sangama dynasty and Śṛṅgeri *maṭha*. It seems that the literature created with a certain purpose in mind lived up to expectations as after some time it was translated into collective memory. The story about the early Sangamas continuing the tradition of old dynasties was successfully connected with sage Vidyāraṇya's figure allegedly continuing the line of great Śaṅkarācārya in Śṛṅgeri. Śṛṅgeri itself received the status of Śaṅkaramaṭha. The fact that this version is still used is the best proof that literary activity can help in creating empires of gods and kings.[139] And Gaṅgādevī definitely has her little share in this enterprise presenting her king as the receiver of the magic indomitable sword inherited from the Pāṇḍyas.

3.6. The battle with the Sultan or plotting against history

The battle which follows the mysterious woman's speech is the culmination of Gaṅgādevī's narration. The fight is fierce: turbaned heads fall, streams of blood form many Tāmraparṇīs, killed warriors attain paradise or *svarga*. The king is a real paragon of heroism. His deeds on the battlefield are described in a conventional manner. With one blow of his sword he splits in two both elephants and their riders with their coat of mail (*ekaprahāreṇa sakaṅkaṭānām ādhoraṇānām karinām ca*—MV Final canto).
Pearls came out from the heads of other elephants pierced with

[139] The Sāluva dynasty lasted perhaps for too short a time for one to be able to expect similar results, i.e. the disappearance of the figure of Kampana as the conqueror of Madhurā Suratrāṇa and taking over the story of triumph over the alien rulers.

his javelin, like flocks of geese from the hole in the Krauñca mountain.[140] The white colour of pearls and geese obviously suggests the king's fame. The pearls coming out from the elephants' globes are mentioned in three more strophes. Perhaps Gaṅgā uses this image also because of its oxymoronic nature: the white colour of pearls and the dark red hue of blood at the battlefield, the coldness of pearls and the warmth of blood are in the same contrast as life and death.

The climax of the battle is the fight between Kampana and Madurai Sultan (*suratrāṇa*). As is required by the *kāvya* convention, the antagonist (*pratināyaka*) is also presented as a powerful and courageous man—indeed, a victory over such an adversary brings fame. Among all the sentences creating a picture of a mighty heir to the throne of the Madurai Sultanate, one calls for attention:

parākramādhaḥkṛtacolapāṇḍyaṃ
vallālasampallatikākuṭhāram /
raṇonmukhaṃ kampanṛpo 'bhyanandīd
vīraḥ suratrāṇam udagraśauryaḥ // MV 9.27 //

The brave hero king Kampana was delighted
having such an opponent in battle as the Sultan,
who by his power reduced the Colas and Pāṇḍyas,
and who was an axe to the creeper of Ballāla's prosperity.

There is no doubt that from this point of view the victory over such an enemy, who had defeated the Colas, Pāṇḍyas and Kākatīyas, was definite proof that the Vijayanagara rulers were the protectors of *dharma*, worthy to be the successors of the splendours of old dynasties. Vijayanagara sovereignty could be fully legitimate.

---

[140] As was believed, the biggest pearls grow in the temples of elephants (*gajamukta*).

At the beginning, the two fighters, Kampana and Sultan, shot arrows at each other. The wounds on Kampana's body caused by the Yavana king's arrows shone like the nail marks of the Goddess of Victory.[141] Finally, Kampana cut the bow string of the Tuluṣka king with his arrows. The time for using swords came. Kampana beheaded the Sultan with his divine sword. The South was finally freed from Pārasīkas (*dig dakṣiṇāsīt kṣatapārasīkā*).

The mortal struggle between Kampana and Qurbat Hasan Kangu has been described in detail in 11 stanzas. What is the real truth, though? The *mahākāvya* or *campū* has special rules governing the depicted world and a license to a special use of language. The language is supposed to give an aura of kingship but no one promises a systematic account of events. Does the choice of a hero who is a contemporary to the author of the literary work in question situate the *mahākāvya* or *campū* within the sphere of history? Or does the historical person chosen as the hero act true to type? That means that Kampana, once offered a magic sword by a supernatural being, has to use it in the next chapter and unavoidably win the combat. There is no doubt that Kampana broke down Muhammadan power in the South, but can one be sure that the Sultan died in a duel with the Vijayanagara viceroy? Or was there a duel that finished with Kampana's victory at all?

According to Shams Siraj Afif's *Tārīkh-i-Fīrūz-Shāhī or History of Fīrūz-Shāh*:

> A neighbouring chief named Bukka at the head of a body of men and elephants marched into Ma'bar and made Qurbat Hasan Kangu prisoner.
> (Thiruvenkatachari 1957: 54)

---

[141] MV, the final canto:
kṣatāni yān yasya śaraiḥ śarīre cakāra vīrasya tuluṣkavīraḥ /
vitenire tāni nakhāṅkaśaṅkām jayaśriyo bhogasamutsukāyāḥ // 31 //
The idea presented here is that the Goddess of Victory is Kampana's lover and it suggests that he will be the winner in this fight.

There are two other *mahākāvyas* that mention the slaying of the Suratrāṇa, but the victory is ascribed to Sāluva Maṅgi, who was the general under Sāvaṇṇa. The inscriptions record such a name even if Gaṅgādevī is silent about it.[142] The authors of the *Rāmābhyudaya* and *Sāluvābhyudaya* speak about the event. The author of the *Rāmābhyudaya*, before telling the story of Rāma, provides us with information concerning the Sāluvas. The authorship of this epic poem is not certain. The majority of scholars generally ascribe it to Sāluva Narasiṃha,[143] the founder of the second Vijayanagara dynasty. However, as will be shown, there is a possibility to assign it to the poet of the famous Ḍiṇḍima family. This episode in the history of the Ḍiṇḍimas seems to be closely connected with the end of the Sangamas and the ascent to Vijayanagara's throne of the Sāluvas, a short-lived dynasty.

Stanza 1.64 in the *Rāmābhyudaya* reads:

tad idam rāmacandrasya caritaṃ tatprasādataḥ /
ucyate tena viduṣā narasiṃhamahībhujā //[144]

This story of Rāmacandra is told
by the wise King Narasiṃha through his kindness.

The sentence can be interpreted both that a king called Narasiṃha is the author of the poem and possibly also that the very same King Narasiṃha is the patron of the poet. It was due to his grace and favour that the story of Rāma was told.

[142] The *Madhurāvijaya* is not complete; some *ślokas*, especially from the last cantos, are missing. However, in my opinion, it is hardly possible for Gaṅgādevī to have mentioned the success of one of the generals of Kampana's army in the battle, even if it had been a historical truth. It is clearly visible that Gaṅgā's *mahākāvya* is a eulogy of Kampana and at the same time propaganda of the military success of Vijayanagara. The victory of a general could be easily ascribed to Kampana as the main 'author' of Vijayanagara victory.

[143] Krishnamachariar 1989: 218; Visalakshy 2003: Introduction 7, 10; Thiruvenkatachari 1957: Introduction 60, Krishnaswami Aiyangar 2003: 32.

[144] Visalakshy 2003: 18.

The pieces of information given by the colophons are even more confusing. The first chapter is closed by the sentence:

RA 1.147cd[145]
viṣṇoḥ śrīnarasiṃhavigrahabhṛto bhāvormisetau kṛtau
śrīrāmābhyudaye 'tra kāvyatilake sargo 'yam ādir gataḥ //

Here ends the opening *sarga*
in the composition *Triumph of Rāma*,
which is an ornament of poetry,
a bridge over the waves of *bhāvas*,
the composition for/of Viṣṇu who takes the form of Narasiṃha.

Again a double interpretation is possible here: the poem is dedicated by the poet to Lord Viṣṇu in his Narasiṃha form or to the King Narasiṃha who is highly praised as the incarnation of Viṣṇu. The other solution, presuming the employment of the genitive sense, opens the possibility of a Narasiṃha being the author of the composition.

To sum up, the colophon gives no certainty who is the author of the poem. There is no usual formula with the instrumental case providing the name of the author responsible for composing (*viracita, nirmita, kṛta*) the work. The message we get from such fragments is obvious—the victories of Narasiṃha Sāluva are comparable to those of Rāma and he himself is compared to Viṣṇu in his Narasiṃha *avatara* (an allusion to the name of the usurper). However, there is no certatinty as to the name of the composer of this poem.

The same formula (with the necessary change of the number of the *sarga* of course) is repeated in the rest of *sargas*. In some chapters an additional colophon appears, perhaps coming from a scribe as it repeats the information given earlier that here the *sarga* ends, i.e.:

---

[145] The first half of the strophe contains the epithets of Viṣṇu Narasiṃha (Visalakshy 2003: 24).

viṣṇoḥ śrīnarasiṃhavigrahabhṛto bhāvormisetau kṛtau
śrīrāmābhyudaye 'tra kāvyatilake sargaś caturtho 'gamat //
iti rāmābhyudaye caturthaḥ sargaḥ /[146]

Of the utmost interest is the end of Chapter 5. After the above-quoted sentence, which besides other interpretations can be read that a person called Narasiṃha is the author of the work, we learn that the son of Rājanātha and Ambābhirāmā, Śoṇādrīndra Ḍiṇḍima, using the titles of Kavīndra and Sārvabhauma, has written the poem—stanza. 5.75! This revelation is "sealed" with a corroborating formula:

iti ḍiṇḍimasārvabhaumakṛtau rāmābhyudaye pañcamaḥ sargaḥ /[147]

Cantos 6, 8, 10, 11, 12 and 16 end with stanzas mentioning Narasiṃha and newly gained knowledge, i.e.

iti ḍiṇḍimasārvabhaumakṛtau śrīrāmābhyudaye ṣaṣṭhaḥ [*aṣṭamaḥ*, etc.] *sargaḥ /*

The remaining cantos are silent about the poet.

The concluding stanza of Chapter 5 gives additional information. The *Rāmābhyudaya* was created before the *Mahānāṭaka*, it was first in succession (*kramaviṣayamhānāṭakasyāgrajāta*). The *Mahānāṭaka* mentioned here is in all probability *Mahānāṭaka-sudhānidhi* in the words of Krishnamachariar (Krishnamachariar 2004: 641), an anthology of the story of *Rāmāyaṇa*, composed by king Devarāya of Vijayanagara. Who was Śoṇādrīndra Ḍiṇḍima? Let us refer to the text again:

śoṇādrīndraṃ kavīndraṃ śravaṇakaṭuraḍḍiṇḍimaṃ sārvabhaumaṃ
prāsūtāmbābhirāmā navanavakavitābhājanaṃ rājanāthāt / RA 5.75ab[148]

---

[146] Visalakshy 2003: 49.

[147] Ibid.: 56.

[148] Ibid.

Ambābhirāmā had with Rājānātha (a son), Śoṇadrīndra,
Lord among the Poets,
Known throughout the world,
Announced by the voice of a drum,
New receptacle of fresh style.

It must be Aruṇagirinātha of the Ḍiṇḍima family who hides under the synonym *śoṇādrīndram*,[149] used by the poet to create the rhyme and because of the metre requirements.

According to a Sanskrit work, the *Vibhāgaratnamālikā*,[150] the ancestor of this family of poets, invited by the Cola kings, migrated from the banks of the Ganges and settled in the village named after its deity Talpagrāma or Rājanāthapura. His skills in composing poetry brought him the right to be announced by the sound of drums (*ḍiṇḍima*) and that is why he and his family were known as Ḍiṇḍima or Gauḍa-Ḍiṇḍima. The rulers of Belur were their patrons. Later on Bukka I granted them the village of Attiyūr. During his reign ten other families moved to Navagrāma. The most important member of the Ḍiṇḍima family was Aruṇagirinātha promoted by Prauḍha Devarāya II (1424–1446), who donated him the village near Navagrāma. The village was known as Mūlāṇḍram or Prauḍhadevapuram, Ḍiṇḍimālayam or Sārvabhaumapuram, as Sārvabhauma Kavi was the title given to Aruṇagirinātha. There are several inscriptions which refer to the family. For instance, Ḍiṇḍima Kavi is mentioned in the Svayambhūnātheśvara temple in Mullaṇḍram. He must have been the poet Aruṇagirinātha Ḍiṇḍima Kavi Sārvabhauma, the hero of a local chronicle (Aiyangar 1942: 27).

---

149 *śoṇa* = *aruṇa*—meaning red colour, dawn; *adri* = *giri*—meaning mountain; *indra* = *nātha*—meaning lord, king. The compound word refers to the deity of Aruṇacala or "Dawn-coloured Mountain". Some connections of the Ḍiṇḍima family with the shrine of Aruṇācala are indicated by their names appearing alternatively as Aruṇagirinātha or Aruṇācaleśvara.

150 The work was edited under the title *Vivekapatramālā* by T. A. Gopinatha Rao in the Indian Antiquary, 1918.

The reign of Devarāya II was the golden age of the Sangama dynasty. In addition to all his victories and successes, his court was a famous cultural centre. Devarāya, himself a scholar and a poet, was a great patron of men of letters. As legend has it, the famous Ḍiṇḍima Kavi was defeated in one of the literary debates by another author at the king's court, namely the famous Telugu poet Śrīnātha. Devarāya is the author of the above-mentioned *campū Mahānāṭaka-sudhānidhi.*[151] So the stanza RA 5.75b gives the priority in time to the *Rāmābhyudaya.* The work of Aruṇagirinātha Ḍiṇḍima, a poet at the king's court, was written before Devarāya's own poem, which is dated around 1440. One has to agree with Visalakshy, the editor of the *Rāmābhyudaya*, that it is highly improbable to make a reference mentioning a subsequent work while writing the book (Visalakshy 2003; 10). The last two lines of verse RA 5.75 should be treated as an interpolation as Visalakshy suggests. She arrives at a conclusion that the whole text must have been composed by king Narasiṃha (reign 1485–1491). However, such a statement does not explain who is responsible for the interpolations. Why would Sāluva Narasiṃha inform about the authorship of Aruṇagirinātha Ḍiṇḍima? If the scribe had made a mistake, why would it happen in so many places? And the remark about the priority of this poem over the work of Devarāya put together with it would be even more surprising.

There is also one fact corroborating the hypothesis that Aruṇagirinātha Ḍiṇḍima could be the author of the *Rāmābhyudaya.* From the prologue to his prahasana *Somavalliyogānanda,*[152] one gains more details concerning the history of the family. We can assume that Aruṇagirinātha's mother was a sister of Sabhāpati. As is known, Sabhāpati was the father of Svayambhu, who mar-

---

[151] Triennial Cat. of Sanskrit Manuscripts in Oriental Library, Madras vol. I. 879; II. 2115, Catalogue of Manuscripts in the Palace Library, Tanjore by P.P.S. Sastri, VIII. 3704.

[152] Triennial Cat. of Sanskrit Manuscripts in Oriental Library, Madras, II. 2276

ried a daughter of Aruṇagirinātha, and he also fathered a daughter Abhirāmakāmākṣi. Abhirāmakāmākṣi was the authoress of *Abhinava-Rāmābhyudaya*[153]—a new *Rāmābhyudaya*. Her close connections with the family of the famous Ḍiṇḍima Kavi Sārvabhauma, the author of the *Rāmābhyudaya*, could make her willing to write a completely new *Rāmābhyudaya*. Her poem about Rāma was divided into 24 cantos, exactly like the previous work under the title of the *Rāmābhyudaya*.

In my opinion, there is one person who could rewrite the poem of Aruṇagirinātha, namely his own son Rājanātha II. His father was a real star in the galaxy of literati at the court of Devarāya II and the bosom friend of this powerful monarch, if we are going to believe the *Vibhāgaratnamālikā*. Rājanātha was a court poet of Narasiṃha, the founder of the new dynasty. After Devarāya's death, the heyday of Sangama rulers was a matter of past. The weak and incompetent rule and fratricidal wars in the family were the causes of the rapid decline of royal power. Vijayanagara lost control over some territories but the southern lands were protected by the trusted commander of a large royal army, Sāluva Narasiṃha. This noble rose in power and prominence, subjugated the Tamil plain, and in 1485 he usurped the throne. As Burton Stein notices:

> His Tamil conquest differed from all previous Vijayanagara forays into the South by setting aside the ancient authority of Tamil kings and chiefs, whom he replaced by a man like himself representing new imperial order.
> (Stein 1997: 71)

However, that man of military and administrative talents, planning to establish a new dynasty, had to surround his family with an aura of kingship. He did not move the capital of the kingdom to

[153] Triennial Cat. of Sanskrit Manuscripts in Oriental Library, Madras vol. IV. 5202.

the more convenient for him and secure Candragiri, his patrimony. The 'City of Victory' was the symbol of the empire. He could have aspired to imitate the example he witnessed himself—the life at the court of Devarāya II. The Ḍiṇḍima poets were connected with the royal house of Vijayanagara from its very beginning, as is attested by a copper plate grant of Bukka I. Definitely, it must have been essential for a new ruler to have a poet or poets coming from this family at his service. Rājanātha, a son of distinguished Aruṇagirinātha Ḍiṇḍima Kavīndra Sārvabhauma, was an ideal candidate to write a panegyrical poem on the king's ancestors and his heroic deeds. It seems that the quickest way to achieve this aim was to rewrite the existent (perhaps unfinished?) poem, or at least its parts, and dedicate it to the new king.[154] It was enough to add information about Narasiṃha and his ancestors to the first canto of the poem and suitable colophons dedicating the poem to the ruler. However, just in the middle of the poem (cantos 5, 6, 8, 10, 11, 12 and 16), there are some colophons ascribing the work to Ḍiṇḍima Sārvabhauma. Did Rājanātha considered it his duty to preserve the name of his father, the author of Rāma's story and the information was put in several somewhat hidden places in the poem, and in the 'external *sargas*' an ambiguous information concerning Narasiṃha authorship was given? It is tempting to put forward such a hypothesis.

The story of Rāma was an interesting subject for the new ruler also from another point of view. Rāma was an incarnation of

[154] The court poet's task was to satisfy his kingly patron, irrespectively of his own feelings. The most telling example in that respect is the life of Amīr Khusrau (1251–1325), the author of the following *qaṣīda*:

> Composing panegyric kills the heart,
> Even if the poetry is fresh and eloquent.
> A lamp is extinguished by a breath,
> Even if it is the breath of Jesus.
> (Sharma 2005: 18)

Viṣṇu, and it is obvious that the composer of the concluding stanzas quoted above plays on the concept of Narasiṃha, the king being an incarnation of Viṣṇu. In that way Narasiṃha's rule could be compared or even equated with the reign of Rāma. Such an idea was fully developed later on in the poem *Raghunāthābhyudaya*. Rāmabhadrāmbā, its authoress, makes "a consistent effort to create for Raghunātha a divine identity that is public, ritualized, and patterned after a specific, dominant paradigm—that of Rāma, epic hero and avatar" (Rao et al. 1998: 192).

For us the most interesting question at the moment is how the ancestors of Narasiṃha Sāluva were introduced. Kampana's campaign against the Muslim rulers in the South is mentioned there and the role of Sāluva Maṅgi, the general who assisted the prince, is stressed. Frankly speaking, Kampana has been marginalised here. It is stated that:

sauhārdāt kamparājasya camburāyā bhayārpakaḥ /
agāj jigīṣus tadarīn agastyayuvatīṃ diśam // RA 1.23 //[155]

Because of his friendship for king Kampana,
the procurer of fear in the Sambhuvarāyas,
striving to conquer his enemies,
went to the southern direction.

As far as we know, Sāluva Maṅgi was an important commander during the campaign against the Madurai Sultanate. Before the fights with Muslims, in the first campaign against the Sambhuvarāyas led by Sāvaṇṇa, he was given the title of *sambhuvarāyasthāpanācārya* (establisher of the Sambhuvarāyas), but never could he be called in such a patronising tone a friend of Vijayanagara prince. He was a general under Kampana's cousin Sāvaṇṇa,[156] not even the commander-in-chief during military operations of both cousins. He was subordinate in rank to Gopaṇa,

[155] Visalakshy 2003: 15.

[156] According to the inscription dated 1369, Sovaṃṇa-Oḍeya was the son of

who was Kampana's general, a fact proved by inscriptions.[157]

In the *Rāmābhyudaya*, he is presented as a victor in the fierce battle (*tasyāsī(t) dakṣiṇasuratrāṇena samaro mahān*—RA 1.24cd) with the Sultan, the one who beheaded him:

svayam tato maṅgidevaḥ suciraṃ racitāhavaḥ /
taddviṣo 'pātayac chittvā [em.; *chitvā* Ed.]
śākaṃ [em.; *sākam* Ed.] *bhuvanapīḍayā* // RA 1.28[158] //

> After a long time, Maṅgideva who waged a war
> because of the compassion for the world,
> decapitated the Śaka himself
> and destroyed his enemies.

According to the *Rāmābhyudaya*, he immortalized his victory over the Muslims by erecting a pillar of victory on the banks of the Tāmraparṇi, then he proceeded to Śrīraṅgam.[159] He presented eight *agrahāras* to the temple, as if to make his conquest of the eight directions memorable, gave away thousand of *sālagrāmas*,

---

Marappa-Oḍeya, the younger brother of Bukka I (Gopal & Ritti 2004: 198, 199). However, there was another Sāvaṇṇa in the Sangama family, namely a son of Kampa I and his successor of Udayagiri Viceroyalty. Sāvaṇṇa's first inscriptions in the Tamil country are dated 1350 and as we know it was him who was engaged in fights with Muslims there and ruled some parts of its territory.

[157] The inscription at Dalavanur, dated 1363 A.D., records an order of Sāluva Maṅgi issued according to a letter from Aṇṇar Gopaṇa (the senior oficer Gopaṇa).

[158] Visalakshy 2003: 15.

[159] *sa nikhāya jayastambhaṃ tāmraparṇītaṭe tataḥ* /
śṛṅgaṃ nirākāragirāṃ śrīraṅgam agaman nṛpaḥ // RA 1.29 //

> After erecting the pillar of victory
> on the bank of the Tāmraparṇī river,
> the king entered Śrīraṅgam,
> the highest expression of Viṣṇu's praise.

together with sixteen other gifts.[160]

The *Sāluvābhyudaya*, in tune with the *Rāmābhyudaya*, says that Sāluva Maṅgi came willing to conquer the Sultan of the South (*dākṣiṇātyam asau suratrāṇam agāj jigīṣuḥ*—SA 1.45ab[161]) and finally he slew him (*ahan suratrāṇam asahyavīrya* (?) *sāluvamaṅgidevaḥ*—SA 1.46ab). It is stated that after the restoration of Hindu rule in Śrīraṅgam, he dispensed one thousand *sālagrāmas*, gave eight *agrahāras* and received the fame and the title of *Śrīraṅgasaṃsthāpana* (SA 1.54–56).

So the ideas presented in the *Rāmābhyudaya* are repeated, sometimes even the same words are used. Of course, in the *Sāluvābhyudaya* the life story of Sāluva Maṅgi is described in a more detailed way, as the whole chapter is dedicated to praise this son of Guṇḍaya, an ancestor of Narasiṃha.

It should be stated that there are no inscriptions corroborating the fact that Maṅgi played such an important role in the campaign against the Madurai Sultanate and restoring order in the Śrīraṅgam temple. On the contrary: there is evidence connecting someone else with the restoration of Śrīraṅgam. It was Gopaṇa, a general of Kampana's army, who played an important role in

---

[160] *sahyajāyāṃ tataḥ snātaḥ sālagrāmasahasradaḥ /*
sākaṃ ṣoḍaśa dānāni tatrākarṣīt sa sāluvaḥ // RA 1.31 //

> Then after a bath in the Kāverī river,
> this Sāluva gave a thousand of *sālagrāmas*
> together with sixteen gifts.

suvṛttān śucibhāvāḍhyān sudṛg yaḥ suguṇottarān /
aṣṭāgrahārān adiśad aṣṭadigvijayī nṛpaḥ // RA 1.32 //

> That well-looking king, a conqueror of eight direction of the world,
> granted eight *agrahāras*, excellent because of their qualities,
> well-conducted and endowed with honest inhabitants.

[161] The text of the *Sāluvābhyudya* comes from the manuscript DC No. 11818 & 11819, Govt. Oriental MSS Library, Chennai.

the reconsecration of the Raṅganātha temple. Maṅgi could not go to Śrīraṅgam just after the decisive battle with the Muslims and find the place flourishing, ready to accept donations and gifts. It probably looked as Gaṅgādevī described it—desolated and ruined. Gopaṇa retook the temples from the Muslims. It is said that deities' festival images were taken by Gopaṇa from Tirupati and for some time kept in Ginjee, his headquarters, and when Śrīraṅgam was freed from the Muslims, Gopaṇa restored the idols. This fact is proved by the inscription on the Śrīraṅgam temple. It is said that on the 17th Vaikasi in the year 1293 of Saṃvat Era—which corresponds to 13th May 1371—Gopaṇa, "the mirror of fame", placed Lord Raṅganātha together with Lakṣmī and Bhū Devī again in their proper place and worshipped them. The tradition ascribes the two stanzas from the Raṅganātha temple to Vedānta Deśika,[162] who on hearing the happy news on the re-established idol, composed the stanzas, which then were inscribed on the temple wall. Other literary sources speak about Gopaṇa's victory over the Muslims (the *Prapannāmṛtam*[163]). The *Kōyil Oḷugu*, which records the history of the Śrīraṅgam temple, describes how he obtained gold from Bukka I with which he purchased 101 villages for the maintenance of the temple.

Is it possible to find the historical truth in the accounts of contemporaries of the heroes or those who lived one hundred years later? It looks as if Kampana's and his commander-in-chief Gopaṇa's fames, once announced by Gaṅgādevī and Vedānta Deśika, were stolen. Such a thing could have happened during the reign of a king who was deeply interested in propagating information about the glorious past of his family in order to show that he and his sons are worth the throne of Vijayanagara. Another clever move was

---

[162] According to Vaishnavite tradition, Vedānta Deśika was born in 1270 and lived for a hundred years. If it is so, the verses must have been composed by him shortly before his death.

[163] For the summary of the *Prapannāmṛtam* of Anantārya and the excerpts from that text see: Aiyangar 2003 (1919): 34–40.

to employ the poet Ḍiṇḍima for the task of writing a panegyric. It could give the sense of continuum of the traditions of Devarāya court and rule. Rājanātha wrote the poem on Sāluva victories, but first the poem about Rāma appeared with its opening *sarga* dedicated to the dynasty legend later on repeated in other literary sources written by the poets of his court.[164] It cannot be proved decisively that it was Rājanātha who is responsible for the interpolations in the work originated some forty years earlier; however, the supposition that its author is Narasiṃha causes more doubts. It is highly improbable that after usurping the Sangamas throne, the at least sixty-year-old experienced commander and administrator would have been devoting his time to writing a poem instead of taking care of the situation in the kingdom. The possibility that he had written the poem during the reign of the Sangamas must be also excluded. How would it be possible to present his own ancestor as more important than the Vijayanagara prince and ascribe him the victory over the Muslims?

3.7. The strategies of telling history

In conclusion, it may be said that these three epic poems, namely *Madhurāvijaya*, *Rāmābhyudaya* and *Sāluvābhyudaya*, are telling examples of how the dynasty legends could have been created. In her poem Gaṅgādevī presents the picture of a *dharmic* king and stresses the fact that the Vijayanagara rulers are the continuators of old dynasties but introducing better methods of management, and their sovereignty is fully accepted by the gods and needed for people and nature.

The tasks of the other two poems are also connected with the

[164] The same information concerning Sāluva Maṅgi is supplied by a Telugu poet at Narasiṃha's court, Pinavīrabhadrudu, the author of *Jaimini Bhāratamu*. For the summary and the excerpts from that text see: Aiyangar 2003 (1919): 29–30, 85–87.

legitimation of the claim to the freshly seized throne. It can be pointed out that some historical events were described by the authors of all these poems in accordance with interests of the rulers, disregarding the historical truth.

The picture of the City as well as Empire of Vijayanagara that we are getting could be described in terms proposed by Robert Redfield and Milton B. Singer for two types of cities: orthogenetic and heterogenetic. The term orthogenetic is explained as "carrying forward into systematic and reflective dimension an old culture", whereas heterogenetic means "creating (...) original modes of thought that have authority beyond or in conflict with old cultures and civilizations".[165] In other words, the first term offers a picture of a place governed by moral order with every representative of social strata in their proper places, and which respects the traditional culture and does not accept innovations and new concepts easily. The other one assumes openness and readiness to participate in the intercultural discourse. Judging by Gaṅgādevī's poem, the Vijayanagara society was closed for strangers and the accomplishments of other cultures, i.e. orthogenetic, inaccessible for those who do not obey Hindu gods and Hindu moral order. However, it seems that it was not the case of the Vijayanagara kingdom and its rulers. In recent years scholars have begun to notice and describe the presence of the process of Islamicization visible in different manifestations of the Vijayanagara culture. The system of men's court dress (Fig. 14) is one of the instances of Islamicization. The transformation of the image of the Vijayanagara king and his courtiers goes together with the change in the political language as it is proved by the adoption of the title *hindu-rāya-suratrāṇa*, literally "Sultan among Hindu

[165] See: Redfield & Singer 1954: 53–73. See also the discussion of the pictures of three cities, namely Ayodhyā from the *Rāmāyaṇa* of Vālmikī, and Pukār and Madurai from the Tamil epic *Cilappatikāram*, in terms of their orthogenetic and heterogenetic features as presented in A. K. Ramanujan's article 'Towards an Anthology of City Images' (Ramanujan 2004).

Kings". It was Bukka I who first used the title.[166] Perhaps it is worth emphasising that the early Sangama rulers did not use the imperial titles of *rājādhirāja* or *rājaparameśvara* but the modest *mahāmaṇḍaleśvara* and *oḍeya* (lord or chief). I agree with Philip Wagoner's suggestion that the title *hindu-rāya-suratrāṇa* would have served to differentiate its bearer from ordinary Hindu (i.e. Indic) kings by signalling his willingness to participate in the political discourse of Islamicate civilization", to use the term introduced by Hodgson.[167] In Wagoner's words:

> Because of the fact that Muslim polities had risen to a position of dominance within much of South Asia by the Vijayanagara period, it was no longer sufficient for a South Indian ruler to articulate his claims to legitimacy solely within a traditional Indic idiom. (Wagoner 1996b: 863)

The question arises: why is this attitude, namely openness and readiness to participate in the transcultural dialogue, not reflected in otherwise quite realistic depiction of the City of Victory as given in the *Madhurāvijaya mahākāvya* authored by Gaṅgādevī, a poetess from the court of Bukka's son? Is the main subject of her poem,[168] namely the conquering the Sultan of Madurai, re-

[166] The epigraphical evidence is listed by Wagoner in his article "Sultan among Hindu Kings: Dress, Titles, and the Islamicisation of Hindu Culture at Vijayanagara", (Wagoner 1996, footnote 8, p. 862. See also the text of Penugonda inscription given in footnote 138, p. 122 of the present monograph).

[167] Hodgson 1974. P. Wagoner explains that the adjective *Islamicate* coined by Hodgson describes the qualities specific to a social and cultural context associated with Islam and Muslims in opposition to the adjective *Islamic* which has religious sense. Similarly Wagoner uses the term *Islamicization* as referring to the process of becoming *Islamicate* whereas *Islamization* pertains to the sphere of religion (Wagoner 1996: 855).

[168] In terms proposed by Richard H. Davies as a response to Aziz Ahmad's classification of literay works of Persian authors as the epics of conquest and those penned by Sanskrit authors as the epics of resistance, the *Madhurāvijaya* could be called a poem of reconquest.

sponsible for that? In fact, Tuluṣkas are depicted in the poem in negative categories: meat-eaters and heavy drinkers, responsible for devastation of Hindu temples, killing Hindu people and cows. The descriptions of Śrīraṅgam, Cidambaram and Madhurā under Muslim rule as given in the poem are negations of the usual role of the city description. Such a presentation can only create dislike for everything which is strange and different and as we know this was not the attitude of Vijayanagara culture. It could be presumed that these xenophobic traits are connected with introducing the description of an enemy. However, in the same poem the campaign against Sambhuvarāya is mentioned and the attitude of the authoress to this local ruler is different—there are no pictures showing his bad conduct and rules. It seems that Islamicization at Vijayanagara was connected with the secular political sphere, whereas the religious culture was influenced by Sanskritic norms of belief, ritual and social behaviour with the dominant role of Brahmanas widely distributing Sanskrit culture. Brahmanas were important to legitimise and sanctify the position of a king and his reign. Velcheru Narayana Rao observes that Brahmanas were conferring the status of *kṣatriya*hood on South Indian kings and these *kṣatriya* kings were making Brahmanas powerful by their patronage.[169] Taking into account this complex relations it can be stated that the kings of Vijayanagara cleverly operated on two distinct fields. In the sphere of Sanskrit culture, their devotion to Sanskritic moral, religious, social norms and Great Tradition is emphasized. The secular sphere is open to the local cultures including Muslim political thought and material culture as well as Dravidian idiom. Perhaps this elasticity and ability to use and change different codes was responsible for the success of the Vijayanagara kingdom. Its rulers had the support of Brahmanas and were recognised as belonging to the world of Sanskrit culture and representing Brahmanical ideology, which brought Vijayanagara

[169] Velcheru Narayana Rao 1995: 25–26.

the label of the "last bastion of Hindu orthodoxy" used so often in modern times. On the other hand, they were open to the norms and usages of Islamicate modes of legitimation and sensitive to the needs of the representatives of the local Dravidian cultures, their subjects. The kings of Vijayanagara patronised Telugu poets and scholars, as is well known.

Coming back to the Sanskrit epic poem *Madhurāvijaya*, it can be stated that its authoress uses the conventions of Sanskrit literature and, in connection with this fact, offers Brahmanical ideology. One could say that the poem represents one of the two codes which created the culture of Vijayanagara: the code responsible for the orthogenetic picture of the Vijayanagara city and Empire, which in fact could be and should be described as heterogenetic. This time, however, the picture one had been offered was of special value: showing the enemy as the stranger threatening "our norms of life" always unites; while, in fact, in the Tamil country, Kampana and his men were foreigners and invaders. It was better then to concentrate on the otherness of Madurai Sultan and behind the convincing pretext of fight with him hide something more important, namely establishing Vijayanagara rule in the Tuṇḍīra region.

According to her testimony of the epoch, Bukka was the architect of the Vijayanagara kingdom, a claim which finds its confirmation in the inscriptions. He aptly showed himself as the continuator of the traditions of old South Indian dynasties. On the other hand, he demonstrated the far-reaching inclusiveness which became specific for Vijayanagara culture and politics. The famous Sravanabelagola inscription, dated 1368, shows him as the pacifier of a dispute between Jainas and Śrīvaiṣṇavas. Bukka explained that there was no difference between the Vaiṣṇava and Jaina religions at all. And he made the parties hold the hands of one another and state that they would protect the interests of both religions (Ritti & Gopal 2004: 175–177). The rulers of Vijayanagara were equally ready to accept the tribal communities,

Muslims and other foreigners with their 'cultural luggage'. Their gods would marry local goddesses and the royal patrons helped the process of acculturation of different communities.

As to the works eulogizing the usurper Narasiṃha's family, the silence about the great past of the Sangama House goes hand in hand with the subtle play, although not so innocent as by the use of certain details it changes the historical framework. If we are going to believe the authors of the poems, we have to admit that these were the Sāluvas who worked out the position of the Vijayanagara kingdom almost from its beginning, and they are entitled to the throne, also because of their moral and heroic qualities. They all lived lives devoted to the protection of *dharma*.

It also seems that a story about a conqueror of a demon/foreigner will always find rewarding audience. After all it is *vijaya/vadha* which matters, not the name of the hero. A narration about a victory belongs to those telling it at the particular moment in time. And those who were telling it, or in whose name it was being told, needed confirmation of their claim to the throne and the consolidating results it could bring. Gaṅgādevī brings to her side the authority of old dynasties, divine intervention[170] and the glory of Kamparāja's *vijaya*. Interestingly enough, she is silent about the very beginnings of the kingdom, the achievements of Harihara and the ancestors of the Sangama brothers. She builds the narrative about the lineage established by Bukka. We do not know if there were some other *mahākāvyas* narrating the exploits of other Sangama brothers and their progeny, but if so, they were not transmitted because of the fact that these were Bukka's sons and grandsons who continued the Sangama dynasty. Gaṅgādevī's

[170] Such a god's intervention in the Cālukyas' history is described by Bilhaṇa. It is said that apart from all misdeeds and treacheries of his elder brother Someśvara, Vikramāditya was reluctant to start a war with him. But Śiva appeared in his dreams and commanded him to destroy his brother. After a victorious battle Vikrama wanted to restore the kingdom to his elder brother, however, Śiva again intervened and forbade the monarch to do so.

story could be propagated by the later Sangamas, and the Sāluvas could as well connect the names of their ancestors with the events mentioned in it. The continuous fights with Muslims could also add to the longevity of this poem.

All the poems discussed here: the *Madhurāvijaya*, *Saluvābhydaya* and *Ramābhyudaya*, show an interesting process of how the poet creates his/her kingly patron and supplies the ideological frame in which the state functions. The creative vision of the Vijayanagara past served many authors to construct the ideology suitable for the circumstances. On occasion it could be a serious interference. As Philip Wagoner writes about the *Rāyavācakamu*, a unique specimen of Telugu historical prose:

> (...) it rejects later Vijayanagara history, not by a mere passive silence, but by an active historiographic construction that expilicitly *denies* the existance of any kings after Krishnadevaraya. (...) This dynastic paradigm is nowhere contradicted in the reminder of the text; Acyutaraya (who in actuality reigned as Krishnadevaraya's successor, from 1529 to 1542) and "Chandramauli" (identity uncertain, but possibly Krishnadevaraya's nephew Sadashivaraya, who nominally ruled from 1542 until the Aravidu takeover) are each mentioned once in passing, but only as Krishnadevaraya's brothers, not as kings. Even more striking is the obliteration of the entire Aravidu line by this historiographic construction.
> (Wagoner 1993: 31–32)

It turns out that Gaṅgādevī, in fact, deserves the name of the annalist of the Vijayanagara kingdom. Her poem reflects the politics of the state ruled by Bukka I with the help of his progeny and provides some information about court life at that time. Obviously, there are things on which she is silent, and some others are exaggerated, with others shown in accordance with established patterns and literary convention; nevertheless, she acquits herself not only as a talented poetess, but also as a writer of a work documenting some aspects of life and events during the reign of Bukka I.

Chapter 4
The Military Sequence and the *nīti* Subjects in the *Madhurāvijaya* from the Point of View of the Theory of Sanskrit Literature

4.1. Victory as the aim of the *mahākāvya*

It seems only logical that an epic poem should concentrate mainly on heroic deeds and victories of its heroes—gods, as well as legendary, mythological and historical characters. According to the descriptions of the epic poem (*mahākāvya*) offered by theoreticians of literature, the victory of the hero is an indispensable element of the structure of each and every representative of this literary genre.

One of the oldest extant definition (*lakṣaṇa*) of the *mahākāvya* genre given by Bhāmaha in his *Kāvyālaṅkāra* treats the triumph of the hero (*nāyakābhyudaya*) as the final element in the consecutive phases (*saṃdhi*) of the action of this literary composition:

mantradūtaprayāṇājināyakābhyudaya[171]

---

[171] KA–Bh 1.20.

> ‘ (. . .) a council, (the dispatch of) an envoy, a march (of an army), a battle, the triumph of the hero.’

This politico-military sequence seems to be an important constituent of the genre never omitted in the treatises discussing the subject.

Also the *Viṣṇudharmottara-purāṇa* gives prominence to it:

> VdhP 15[172]
> *nibaddhau yatra rājendra nāyakapratināyakau // 3 //*
> *prayāṇodyatasaṃpreṣyayuddhayuktaṃ tad eva tu /*
> *nāyakābhyudayopetaṃ mahākāvyaṃ tad iṣyate // 4 //*
>
> It is required from the *mahākāvya* to contain a protagonist and antagonist and provide (the descriptions) of marches undertaken, the dispatch (of an envoy), the fight and the triumph of the hero.

In the detailed definitions of later theoreticians, the sequence also exists, although it is put among a whole list of different subjects and items which should be described in the *mahākāvya.*

> KA–D.
> (. . .) *mahākāvya* (. . .) // 14 //
> *nagarārṇavaśailartucandrārkodayavarṇanaiḥ /*
> *udyānasalilakrīḍāmadhupānaratotsavaiḥ // 16 //*
> *vipralambhair vivāhaiś ca kumārodayavarṇanaiḥ /*
> *mantradūtaprayāṇājināyakābhyudayair api // 17 //*
> *alaṃkṛtam* (. . .) // 18 //
>
> (. . .) the *mahākāvya* (. . .) is ornamented with descriptions of: a city, the ocean, a mountain, seasons, moonrise, sunrise; play in a garden, play in water, drinking wine, the delights of love-making; separations of lovers and weddings, the birth/ the growing up of sons; and also a council, (the dispatch of) an envoy, a march (of an army), a battle, the victory of the hero (. . .).[173]

---

172 *Viṣṇudharmottara-purāṇa* Third Khaṇḍa (Shah 1958: 33–34).

173 Transl. Trynkowska 2000: 40.

It seems that the 'classical' *mahākāvya* speaks about the victory of the hero over a demon, which can be viewed as the reworking of an archetypal motif of a god overcoming chaos. The deadly fight not only saves the world from the destruction, but also brings the renewal of the moral order, and with it the revitalization of kingly power. This is the case of the *mahākāvyas* based on mythological stories, the *Rāmāyaṇa* and the plots taken from the *Mahābhārata*.

However, at a certain moment, the so-called historical Sanskrit epic poems appear on the scene, and it turns out that elements such as battles and victories of kings could be desired and useful in building the image of a warrior-king. In South India it could go hand in hand with the construction of medieval polity based on the web of military associations. As Cynthia Talbot points out:

> (...) kingship in medieval South India was not just about being a good warrior, either in theory of practice. But military action was a very substantial element in both the success of actual kings and in the ways people thought about kings, and, as such, merits far more consideration than it has hitherto received from historians of South India. (...) While divine legitimation and the support of institutionalized religion were important assets to royal authority, they could never constitute its fundamental ground. Even donative inscriptions, which by their nature as records of religious endowments magnify religious dimensions over other aspects of society, reveal the ideological premium placed on martial heroism as a royal attribute and highlight the bonds of military service uniting leading warriors.
> (Talbot 2001: 144)

4.2. Before the battle: *mantra*, *dūta* and *prayāṇa*

The component inseparable from the fight and inescapable victory is the march of the hero's army or *prayāṇa*. *Mahākāvya* poets use the moment of the king's setting out with his army to show the picture of his capital city and its inhabitants, and their reaction to the view of the brave king with his warriors; especially the excitement of womenfolk is shown in great detail. The army passes through the rivers, mountains and forests of the country and very often the autumnal landscape constitutes the background for the hero on the march. Indeed, because of practical reasons it was convenient to start the military campaign at this time of the year: with streams and rivers shrinking back to their old channels after heavy rains, passable roads, plenty of food as it is harvest time, and agreeable weather. But the poets emphasise the white colour as the dominating feature of autumn: again the lakes and rivers are full of blossoming white lotuses and the whiteness of migratory birds is described. The characteristics of autumn could have been used by writers to suggest the future victory of a hero as according to the convention the colour was associated with fame. The poets, while describing the moving army, usually show off their knowledge of military science. If the setting up of a camp is mentioned, the poets' preferences go for the descriptions of nights with drinking and love-making.

Even if the sequence a *march of an army/a battle/ the victory* of the hero is present in the poems, and one has to admit that in the majority of *mahākāvyas* it does appear, the council (*mantra*) and sending an envoy (*dūta*) are not always described. These are, however, significant constituents of the genre as they usually form discursive parts of the *māhakāvya*. The epic poems containing the most famous *mantra* episodes were discussed in different treatises on the *alaṃkāraśāstra*. The speeches delivered at councils and the speeches of envoys were the subject of analysis even in the poems themselves. From Bhāravi's *Kirātārjunīya*, for instance, the reader or listener can learn what a good speech should be like (KA 2.1; 2.5; 11.38–40; 14.3–4). Besides, some of the speeches discuss the issues concerning the art of politics—*nītiśāstra*.

The whole sequence mentioned by Bhāmaha and later theoreticians of Sanskrit literature appears only in certain *mahākāvyas*, although very often the *kāvya* authors evidently substitute its elements, giving some equivalents. This is the case of Aśvaghoṣas's poems. David Smith labels *Buddhacarita* (Acts of the Buddha) "an anti-court epic, for much of it concerns Buddha's voluntary renunciation of court life".[174] Similarly, his *Saundarananda* (Handsome Nanda) shows Nanda's renunciation of the pleasures of courtly life. The choice of heroes obviously prevents the appearance of the military sequence, but in the case of these two poems and some other *mahākāvyas* their composers offer certain adequate situations. To name just a few: in the *Buddhacarita* Gautama wins the battle with Māra and becomes the Buddha; Nanda fights with his attachment to worldly pleasures and finally obtains *arhat*ship; in the *Kumārasaṃbhava* (The Birth of Kumāra) it is Parvatī who, engaged in severe austerities, wins her "battle", i.e. becomes Śiva's wife.[175]

4.3. Poetess Gaṅgādevī's execution of the political-military plot

4.3.a. Counsel and embassies constituents substituted

In the earlier chapters Gaṅgādevī's way of telling history was discussed and pieces of historical information were sought. However, as a representative of the *mahākāvya* genre belonging to *kāvya* tradition, her poem should be evaluated in terms proper for its kind. Its structure and stylistics was governed by the rules meticulously presented by different theoreticians of Sanskrit literature. It goes

[174] Smith 1985: 25.

[175] More about the execution of the political military sequence in early *mahākāvyas* in: Sudyka 2003.

without saying that the widely accepted pan-Indian poetical practice shaped the narration of Gaṅgā. Since her treatment of *śṛṅgāra* themes was already discussed, it would be recommended to concentrate once again on the political-military sequence as presented in her work, this time leaving aside the problems of historicity or creation of dynastic legends.

It is already well-known that a march of the army, a battle and the triumph of the hero belong to Gaṅgā's story, a fact which is even suggested by the title *Madhurā-**vijaya***. We also know that Prince Kampana was sent by his father to fight. However, there is no such conventional element of the plot as despatching an envoy unless we consider Kampana as an ambassador of his father, announcing the aim of his mission—to enlarge the Vijayanagara kingdom territory and strengthen its position. There is no description of a counsel as well but Kampana hears about the deeds of the foe form the mouth of his father and at the same time he is given by King Bukka all kinds of instructions and advice, which triggers off a chain of future events. So as in the pattern described by Vladimir Propp for magic tales, right at the moment when misfortune or lack is made known, the counter-action is undertaken. This is a crucial decision for the hero that sets the course of action and with it he takes on the mantle of heroism. One can believe that a figure of a spy usually informing about the danger was replaced with a persona of the king explaining to his son why he should undertake the action without delay. Then the mysterious woman plays exactly the same role.

So the *Madhurāvijaya* does not contain *mantra* and *dūta* episodes. However, there are discursive passages in it which substitute for the council theme, make up for the enyoy's speeches, and in that way fulfil the requirements of the genre, in which the dialogic parts are expected and the treatment of certain subjects in them is prescribed.

The battle with Sambhuvarāya is preceded by King Bukka's speech, and the oration of the mysterious woman urges Kampana to start a fight with the Sultan. Both speeches could be compared with the oration of Draupadī delivered during the counsel described in the *Kirātārjunīya*. All of them create a sort of lament over the dramatic situation and challenge the addressees of the speeches to take immediate counteraction. However, Draupadī supports her arguments with the science of politics, which is not the case with the talks contained in the *Madhurāvijaya*. The unnamed woman, as was discussed above, delivers a speech stirring religious issues and displaying a dangerous otherness. King Bukka appeals as a father to his son, and now we are going to concentrate on this aspect. This speech is set in the family context. We see a father who wants his youthful son to be a man of great worth and not to take the wrong path due to the passions of youth. Only due to the instructions of their *guru*s are wise men able to give up the darkness, the consequence of youthfulness, explains Bukka (MV 3.21–22). Youth is like a deep night (*mahāniśīthinī*), the darkness is created by sexual desire (*madāndhakāra)*, and the black colour causes an obstruction to the moon of awakening (*prabodhacandrapratirodhakālikā*), he continues (MV 3.24). "Whose perception in juvenility or the darkness of night is immediate and correct?" (*tamaḥpradoṣe taruṇimni kasya vā samañjasaṃ paśyati dṛṣṭir añjasā*—MV 3.25b), asks King Bukka. In his speech there are also a few sentences concerning the statecraft.

> *dunoti daṇḍena durutsahena yaḥ*
> *prasahya rāṣṭraṃ padam ātmasaṃpadam* /
> *sa vṛkṣam āruhya kuṭhārapātanaṃ*
> *karoti mūloddalanāya durmatiḥ* // MV 3.32 //

> He, who with punishments difficult to bear
> exceedingly torments the subjects—his own wealth —
> is a fool causing an axe to fall with the purpose to cut
> the tree which he climbed up.

Yet another stanza compares the vices of the monarchs to an illness of consumptive nature:[176]

athaibhir aiśvaryaśarīrayakṣmabhir
hatākhilāṅgair vyasanair upadrutāḥ /
tamaḥparābhūtanijaujaso nṛpāḥ
prayānti kālād dviṣatām upekṣyatām // MV 3.34 //

> The ignorance-afflicted kings, affected by these vices,
> which are like consumptions for the body of kingly power,
> in the course of time, gain disregard of their foes.

Then Bukka points out that intelligent young men like his son, thanks to the instructions of their *gurus* and their nature, are capable of acting properly and rejecting evil (MV 3.36). And the king adds that he should act in this way since "the always unsteady Goddess of Royal Fortune continually follows the stage of constancy because of your qualities" (*yatheyam ekāntacalā bhavad-guṇair labheta lakṣmīḥ sthiratām anāratam* // MV 3.37cd).

Only after the 17-stanza-long speech does he reach the gist of it. In three next verses he explains the necessity of waging war against enemies (MV 3.38–40). And the couplets 41–43 name the foes which are Sambhuvarāya and demoniac Turuṣka.

The speech of the mysterious lady in canto 8 can, in fact, be treated as connected with the first address delivered by King Bukka. She reminds Kampana, indulged in royal enjoyments, of the second part of his father's order.

In this way both speeches make Kampana not only the head of the army and the hero, but also an obedient son, which is the right path to follow.

---

[176] This stanza contains a conceptual metaphor, which, according to Anna Trynkowska's analysis of Sanskrit *mahākāvyas*, carried on with the methods of cognitive linguistics, belongs to the category THE APPROPRIATE CONDITION OF THE STATE IS THE APPROPRIATE CONDITION OF THE HUMAN BODY (Trynkowska, forthcoming).

4.3.b. A march of an army and battle

As far as we know, the destruction of the Sambhuvarāyas and the Madurai Sultanate were presented by Gaṅgādevī as two aspects of a far-reaching plan aimied at destroying Muslims and reintroducing Hindu *dharma* in the Tamil country. Perhaps such a presentation has very little to do with the real situation, as mentioned above. Now, however, we are going to concentrate on the author's imagery of the battle scenes.

First of all, it must be stated that the battles are described in two cantos: 4 and the concluding, unfortunately incomplete one, which in the edition of Thiruvenkatachari is not numbered.[177] Canto 4 consists of 83 stanzas. The first 16 stanzas of *sarga* 4 are devoted to the depiction of dawn in a military camp. In the *Harṣacarita* of Bāṇa, the military expedition of King Harṣa against the Gauda king also starts in the morning, a fact which enables the poet to show the activities of soldiers and the animals in connection with both occasions described there—the beginning of a military campaign and the beginning of the day. As Rajendran C. points out in his article *Business unusual: Bāṇa's description of Dawn in Harṣacarita*:

> Bāṇa's description of the dawn in the army camp is interesting in that it does not include any of the stereotyped images usually associated with dawn in classical Sanskrit poetry like the blossoming of the lotuses or the shrinking of the water lilies, the conduct of waking lovers and the like. It is purely functional and context oriented. Dawn is here regarded as the appropriate moment to start expedition, and it is business unusual for people in the camp and the animals engaged in fight and transportation. There is commotion and excitement in the air as the entire camp readies for the onward march.
> (Rajendran 2008: 144)

[177] One cannot be certain if this fragmentarily preserved chapter was really following canto 8.

As Rajendran suggested, Bāṇa could afford to be strictly functional in his approach to the descriptions as his composition belongs to the *ākhyāyikā* genre. He was not bound by the strict rules provided by the theoreticians of literature as is the case with another type of literary composition, namely the *sargabandha mahākāvya*, which can also, at least one of its subtypes—the so-called historical *mahākāvya*—pretend to be a kind of biography.

Gaṅgādevī, although the authoress of a *sargabandha mahākāvya*, does not pay too much attention to the conventional images and natural phenomena associated with the dawn and so often recalled in the epic poems. In 34 stanzas describing the preparations for the march undertaken in the morning, there are only four couplets referring to the fact that all the activities take part at that time of the day. These are above all the first two *śloka*s opening the canto:

anyedyur atha rājīvavanajīvanadāyini /
lokaikadīpe bhagavatyudite bhānumālini // MV 4.1 //
vihāya nidrāṃ vidhivan nirmitāharmukhakriyaḥ /
ādikṣat pṛtanādhyakṣān senāsannahanāya saḥ // MV 4.2 //

> When the glorious sun—
> a gardener granting life to the clusters of lotuses,
> the single lamp for the universe—rose up the next day,
> he (Kampana) woke up from sleep
> and after duly performing the rites
> prescribed for the beginning of the day,
> ordered his generals to get the army ready for fight.

The following stanzas give the setting of the event: it is dawn in the capital city. The poetess uses conventional images: on the one side we have a crown prince starting the day with proper rites, then giving orders, and on the other side, there is the sun, which, with its beams, opens lotuses and water lilies blossoming during the daytime. It can be said that the most important figures appear on the scene: those who animate the world of plants, animals and people, as we see. The other couplets offer only some hints as to this particular time of the day: umbrellas resembling white lotuses in the river of the army (MV 4.12), the rays of the rising sun which cannot leave their redness because of the sparkling gems of the kings (MV 4.14), and Aruṇa, the charioteer, who, because of the flags, is in difficulty while riding the chariot of the sun (MV 4.15).

Unlike Bāṇa, Gaṅgādevī is not systematic in her presentation of the consecutive stages of the preparations for the march. It seems that Gaṅgādevī chooses certain images and develops the scenes which caught her attention as a poet. She is not very much interested in the military aspects of the event. Of course, as the author of a *mahākāvya* she should also present her knowledge about these aspects of statecraft and military science. And that is what she does, although within a very limited space. She describes the divisions of the army in four stanzas:

ābaddhakuthamātaṅgam āttaparyāṇasaindhavam /
saṃvarmitabhaṭaṃ sadyaḥ samanahyata tadbalam // MV 4.7 //

His army at once got ready:
elephants with the cloth on their back,
saddled horses and
the foot soldiers fully armed.

Then each of three units of the army is briefly characterized: from the massive temples of war-elephants streams ichor, and the horses with foaming mouths, swift as wind, were like the waves in the army-ocean. The general characteristic of infantry is also given:

kṛpāṇakarpaṇaprāsakuntakodaṇḍapāṇayaḥ /
samagacchanta sahasā naikadeśyāḥ padātayaḥ // MV 4.10 //

The foot soldiers from different countries
armed with swords, spears, missiles, lances and bows
gathered immediately.

The motives which receive more attention evidently are connected with the figure of Kampana. The stanzas MV 4.11–15 inform about the kings of neighbouring countries who assembled near the gates, with their white umbrellas, flags and gem studded crowns on their heads, waiting for their suzerain to appear. Finally, they saw Kampana and greeted him with shouts of joy (MV 4.32). A lot of attention is given to the delineation of Kampana's horse (MV 4.20–29). No wonder for, as is well known, horses were important and very much desired in the Vijayanagara kingdom. The king's horse had a symbolic significance in the consecration of his kingship during the Mahānavamī festival (Stein 1980: 387). Domingo Paes writes:

> You must know that this horse that is conducted with all this state is a horse that the king keeps, on which they are sworn and received as kings, and on it must be sworn all those that shall come after them; and in case such a horse dies they put another in its place. (Sewell 1992: 272)

There was a great demand for horses for military purposes, and a supply of strong horses must have been an instrument of political control by Vijayanagara rulers. The clever use of the cavalry, perhaps learned from the Muslims, was one of the reasons for their military success.

So the detailed description of Kampana's horse has its cultural background but, of course, also literary value and even literary parallels, as will be shown below.

The tall horse was waiting for the crown prince near the gates. The speed of the animal is mentioned in several verses. The horse is called a friend of Vāyu and Garuḍa; the wind in fact seemed to be his pupil, taking lessons in speed. He was exceeding even the horse of Indra in speed. A nice comparison to Garuḍa is offered in couplet 25:

mukhalīnakhalīnāhir acchapalyayanacchadaḥ /
vapuṣāpi garutmantam anugantum ivotsukaḥ // MV 4.25 //

He was desirous to imitate Garuḍa also in his bodily form—
with the bit of bridle clinging to his mouth like a snake
and a bright wing-like saddle.

Again we can point to the literary legacy of Bāṇa as offering a certain parallel to that image of a horse. In the *Kādambarī*, Candrāpiḍa's horse is described at length. Bāṇa compares Indrāyuddha to a young elephant, then he says that the animal was "like the bull of Śiva the Destroyer, ruddy with red lead dust from butting the sides of Kailāsa; like Pārvatī's lion with its mane reddened with streaks of clotted blood from the buffalo demon" (Smith 2006: 86). All this suggests the strength and height of the animal and shows the picture in colour. David Smith notices that Bāṇa's comparisons of one animal to another are striking, and "The strongest and richest of such animal composite pictures in Kādambarī is given in the case of prince Candrāpiḍa's horse, Indrāyuddha" (Smith 2006: 86).

In Gaṅgādevī's poem we also have a comparison of Kampana's steed to other animals, namely Indra's horse and an eagle-like creature, i.e. Garuḍa, and the picture, accordingly to the dawn scenery, is painted in bright and reddish colours, too. Uchaiḥśravas, Indra's winged horse, is pure white in colour. Garuḍa is depicted as having a white face, the golden body of a man and red wings.

In the *Madhurāvijaya*, there are also some pictures based on the observation of a natural horse's behaviour,[178] this, however, serves as the basis for metaphors promoting Kampana's fame:

muhuḥ svajavasaṃrodhanamitonnamitānanaḥ /
namaskurvann iva purovartinīṃ vijayaśriyam // MV 4.27 //

(The horse) repeatedly raising and lowering his head
as a result of restraining his speed,
seemed to bow down to the goddess of victory before him.

[178] The realistic description of horses' behaviour at dawn is provided in the *Harṣacarita* (Rajendran 2007: 142–143).

Finally the army sets out. The moment of leaving the city is marked only by one stanza:

ācāralājaiḥ paurāṇāṃ purandhyas tam avākiran /
ambhasāṃ bindubhiḥ śubhrair[179] abhramālā ivācalam // MV 4.33

The wives of townsmen
showered the customary parched rice on him,
like a line of clouds in the sky
pouring bright drops of water on a mountain.

What now, in connection with the marching army, occupies the imagination of the poetess enormously is the dust raised by the moving army. Kampana is compared to the eastern wind (MV IV. 35). The dust created by his army hides the sun, which disappears (MV 4.39). Grains of dust are everywhere—they cover elephants, enter the glands with ichor, are caught by the temples of elephants (MV 4.40, 45); water drops sprayed out from the elephants' trunks absorbing particles of dust shape a kind of hail (MV 4.42), or dust is fanned out by their big ears (MV 4.43). The dust, on the one hand, restrains the fame of the enemy and, on the other, acts as a fertilizer of Kampana's own fame:

tasya dikṣu prarohantyāḥ śatadhā kīrtivīrudhaḥ /
vitatāna rajasstomaḥ karīṣanikarabhramam // MV 4.38 //

The cumulation of dust filled up all the directions
with rolling heaps of cow-dung
for the creeper of his fame shooting forth hundredfold.

prasṛtais taccamūdhūlistomaiḥ kṣīrataraṅgiṇī /
kīrttyā campakṣitīndrasya sākaṃ kaluṣatām agāt // MV 4.49 //

---

[179] In the Thiruvenkatachari's edition: *śumrer* (Thiruvenkatachari 1959: 94); Harihara Sastri and V. Srinivasa Sastri give: *śubhrair* (Sastri & Sastri 1924: 20).

> The multitude of the dust raised by his army
> soiled the Kṣīrataraṅgiṇī (the Pālār river)
> together with the fame of Campa King (Sambuvarāya).

Ten stanzas altogether are dedicated to the motif of dust raised by the king's army marching against the Sambhuvarāya. Four of them are connected with the picture of elephants covered with it, and three couplets deal with the subject of the royal fame of the future victor as well as his enemy.

It is remarkable for this scene of the marching army that it concentrates mainly on the accurate presentation of the animals: elephants and horses. The military landscape is painted in reddish colours. This is the colour of omnipresent dust,[180] the rays of the sun at dawn are of this colour as well, the gems set in kings' crowns are of red hue, and also it must be the tinge of Kampana's steed's saddle. To this red-coloured background the dazzling white spots are added—the umbrellas resembling white lotuses (MV 4.12) and flywhisks reminiscent of geese (MV 4.13). The subject of dawn has been hardly touched, although the colour scheme is proper for the depiction of this part of the day in a Sanskrit *mahākāvya*. To the visual representation of the army getting ready for a march and then marching, Gaṅgādevī adds also sound effects provided by alliterations. The war-drums (*dundubhi*) beaten by drum-sticks (*koṇa*) sounded:

rarāṇa koṇābhihito raṇaniryāṇadundubhiḥ / MV 4.3b

The next three stanzas inform about the intensity of the sound and echoes from the caverns. It is not certain from which place Kampana started his campaign against the Sambhuvarāyas. Gaṅgādevī's narration suggests that it was the City of Victory as in the first canto its description is given. If we think about the possible

[180] It should be pointed out that Gaṅgādevī uses different synonyms for the dust. These are: *rajas*, *parāga*, *dhūli*, *reṇu*, *kṣoda* and *pāṃsu*.

dates of the first and even the second campaign, the Vijayanagara city was not yet built, although at that time Bukka I could already have been ruling from Hosapaṭṭaṇa. In that case the physical surroundings would be identical—a hilly place, with massive boulders and the caves in the hills which echoed with the sound of war-drums. To that noise all the sounds produced by animals—the horses and elephants—contributed:

poṣito hayaheṣābhir bṛṃhito gajabṛṃhitaiḥ /
vardhitas tūryanidhvānaiḥ ko'pi kolāhalo 'bhavat // MV 4.16 //

> The clamour supported by neighing of the horses,
> increased by trumpeting of the elephants and strengthened
> by the sounds of musical instruments was inconceivable

Also people were shouting, as the already-mentioned kings awaiting Kampana near the outer gates, and the Brahmanas were chanting hymns. As is already visible from the stanzas quoted, the poetess employs onomatopoeic words, trying to bring the sound effects of the instruments and animals.

Then, for a moment, Gaṅgādevī tries to be more of an annalist than a poet. She gives information about the route of the army already discussed in chapter 3. The description of a combat again applies conventional stylistics, although sometimes the clash between some elements constructing the images is surprising. For instance, the faces of soldiers cut off by *bhalla* arrows or missiles are compared to lotuses in the river of blood (MV 4.58);[181] or the sparks struck by the clash of weapons are said to be reminiscent of a group of glow-worms in the darkness of the dust.[182]

Also the picture presented in stanza 61 is quite unusual:

vīrāḥ kuñjarakumbheṣu śāyinaḥ śatrusāyakaiḥ /
prābudhyanta surastrīṇāṃ kucakumbheṣu tatkṣaṇāt // MV 4.61 //

---

[181] This particular stanza will be discussed in the next chapter.

[182] *rajastamasi vīrāstrasaṅghasaṃghaṭṭanotthitaiḥ /*
babhre sphuliṅgasaṃghātaiḥ khadyotanivahadyutiḥ // MV 4.55 //

The heroes, put to sleep
on the protrusions of their elephants by enemy arrows,
in a moment woke up
on the pitcher-like breasts of divine ladies.

The fights are described in ten consecutive stanzas (MV 4.52–61). The next five verses (MV 4.62–66) inform about fleeing of the forces of the king of Dravidas (*dramiḍendra*). Some of the soldiers swore that they would never fight again, some others pretended to be dead; however, because of the fear of jackals, they decided to continue their run. Yet others mistook their own shadows for the pursuing enemy. Then Kampana began to lay siege to the stronghold Rājagambhīra, as we already know (MV 4.67). In nine stanzas (MV 4.69–77) the picture of the fortress and its defenders is given. With its flags the stronghold made impression of greeting Kampana, the houses lit up by the missiles were like lamps ready for the ceremony celebrating the victory of the Vijayanagara forces. The stones sent from the fortress' catapults were like messengers. Heads severed by arrows resembled palmyra fruits, and when they were falling down they looked like balls of the deity of war. The comparison of severed heads to fruit is also present in the *Vikramāṅkadevacaritam* of Bilhaṇa.[183] There were pregnant women in the fortress whose embryos slipped out from the mothers' wombs because of fear of the soldiers:

athodbhaṭabhaṭakṣveḍāgalitabhrūṇagārbhiṇam /
nihatāsranadīmajjajjanatāśāsyajīvitam // MV 4.75 //
......
alabdhanirgamaṃ durgam āsīd evam upadrutam // MV 4.76 //

The fortress was oppressed—with no chances for escape,
with its preganat women loosing their embryos
because of battle cries of vehement warriors,
with people immersed in rivers of blood of the slain
but desirous for life.

[183] *adhiruhya baladvaye balād bhujadaṇḍaiḥ paridolanodyate /*
samaradrumataḥ phalāvalir nipapāteva śiraḥkadambakaiḥ // VC 15.44 //

Finally, the decisive fight between the Sambhuvarāya monarch and Kampana took place. It is described in three stanzas, one of which again brings out the idea of pregnancy:

antarbimbitacampendrā kampendrasyāsiputrikā /
apsarobhyaḥ patiṃ dātum antarvatnī kilābhavat // MV 4.81 //

The sword of king Kampa
reflecting the image of Campa monarch
was like a pregnant daughter
about to give (birth to) a husband for *apsaras*es

The analysis of the most important battle for Kampana, the Vijayanagara kingdom and also for this composition, i.e. the fight with the Sultan, must be limited to 40 stanzas only as the rest is unfortunately lost or incomplete. The technique of depiction the poetess is now using is similar. A complex panorama of the battle is built by a series of miniatures showing different scenes. Each of them has a different hero or heroes. A certain warrior pierced with a lance, with the same lance sticking in his body wounded his own oppressor (MV 12[184]). Two warriors, after a long fight, cut each other's heads with their swords (stanza 13). There are also portraits of animals. The war-elephants are depicted or mentioned in 12 strophes. Three of them use the conventional image of pearls obtained from the temples of elephants (stanzas 4, 6, 17). There is also a picture of a dead elephant in whose body the birds of prey are feasting and the corpse moves, which gives impression that the animal lives and the jackals flee away (stanza 7). On the battlefield, there appear also demons drinking the blood of elephants and spitting the pearls (stanza 6), and the severed heads serve the *rākṣasa* women as wreaths ornamenting their ears (stanza 8).

[184] The stanzas of the concluding, unnumbered chapter of the *Madhurāvijaya* in the texts edited by Thiruvenkatachari and Harihara Sastri & Srinivasa Sastri do not have numbers either. For the sake of convenience, I number every stanza, even if incomplete.

Figure 14: Painting of the *raṅga maṇḍapa* ceiling in Lepakshi Temple, Andhra Pradesh. (Photo L. Sudyka)

Figure 15: Hero stone, Penukonda. (Photo L. Sudyka)

The imagery employed here again belongs to the realm of warrior tales, as we know them from Indian textual traditions—headless warriors, demons or goblins haunting the battlefields, pools and rivers of blood, *apsarases* taking the heroes to heaven, comparison of royal warriors to lions (stanza 14), etc. Such heroic stories had their visual representation on the hero stones found all over India, although their largest concentration is in the South India.[185]

The fallen hero is shown with a bow and arrows or riding a horse or elephant and fighting enemies. Some hero stones have three panels: the lowest presents the hero in the battle, the middle one shows him with divine damsels, whereas the uppermost one depicts him adoring his patron deity, very often with the sun and the moon above as representing everlasting fame of the deeds of the hero (Fig. 15).

The association between warriors and lions, as it is observed in stanza 14 of the *Madhurāvijaya* conluding canto, is one of particular interest:

saṅgrāmav anyām abhitaś caranto
***darpoddhatāḥ** kecana **rājasiṃhāḥ** /*
*pratyarthināṃ **pārthivakuñjarāṇāṃ***
śirāṃsy abhindan nakharaiḥ [kharāgraiḥ //]

<In their war madness> <certain kingly warriors>,
wandered all around the battlefield
and tore the heads of their <powerful> adversaries
with their sharp nails,
like <the kings among lions> <aroused by (the smell) of ichor>
do to the mighty elephants.

At first glance the poetical figure employed here is *rūpaka*, i.e. metaphorical identification, then the presence of *śleṣa* or double-entendre comes out into the open. The main idea of *rūpaka* is that

[185] More about hero stones in: Settar & Sontheimer 1982, Vassilkov 2011, Świdzińska 2003 and Świdzińska 2007.

the fighting kings are similar to lions when they encounter their powerful enemies. Here comes the use of *śleṣa*, which I marked both in the original text and its translation. The compound word *rājasiṃha* I read twice: 'the kings-lions' and 'the kings among lions'. The lions are excited by the temporine's (also called ichor) smell (Skr. *darpa*—'musk'), produced by the elephants in rut. The warriors are excited by combat (Skr. *darpa*—'pride, arrogance, haughtiness, insolence, conceit'; in the given context I interpret the compound *darpoddhata* as describing the state of battle frenzy). In *kāvya* convention lions are shown as enemies of elephants[186]—they claw the heads of the latter. And the group of warriors described by Gaṅgādevī behaves exactly the same towards their powerful opponents equated with 'the kings among elephants'.

This image could be treated just as elaborate *kāvya* metaphor strengthened by the presence of paronomasia, showing atrocities of war, and the compund *rājasiṃha* as eulogising and idealizing the hero. However, in this case, as well as in the case of frightening lion-cries of warriors[187] mentioned in MV 4.75–76,[188] it would be possible to point out the possible sources of the origin of these images. According to Yaroslav Vassilkov's research,[189] the epithets such as 'tiger-man' (*puruṣavyāghra*) or 'lion-man' (*narasiṃha*), referring to warriors, can be traced to the animal symbolism of archaic Indo-Aryan warrior brotherhood. Memories of such warrior societies, as Vassilkov claims, are preserved in the *Mahābhārata*:

> Generally speaking, in the MBh, as it seems, there is a cultural layer which shares certain values with the culture of Deccan militant pastoralists—the culture that produced the phenomenon of hero

[186] The most common conventional image is as follows: the lions tear elephants' globes and pearls scatter from their victims' heads.

[187] According to Monier Monier-Williams dictionary, the word *kṣveḍā* among other designations can also mean: 'the roaring of a lion' or 'battle-cry' (Monier-Williams 2005: 334).

[188] For the translation see page 161 of the present monograph.

[189] Vassilkov 2011; Vassilkov forthcomnig a); Vassilkov forthcoming b).

> stones. This may look strange, and one may ask: what link can there be between the Sanskrit epic and these Deccan pastoralist tribal communities? And the answer will be: the Vrātya traditions, the Vrātya culture.
>
> What I mean by the Vrātya culture here is the original, typologically earliest, archaic culture of the Indo-Aryans. The "Vrātya society" is a society of mobile and militant pastoralists, a society characterized by the age-group system and by what J. Heesterman called the "dualistic system of cyclical exchange"—which included the exchange of cattle-raids. The warriors formed militant brotherhoods. In the way similar to other IE peoples, these warrior brotherhoods were of two kinds. One of them were bands of young, adolescent warriors, characterized by aggressiveness and behavior reversed from the norm—they prowled at night, attacked from ambush; were engaged in predatory activities and probably imitated wolfs in their behavior. There were also brotherhoods of adult, married warriors, in whose activities the defensive, "doggish" function probably dominated over the "wolfish", aggressive one.
> (Vassilkov forthcoming a)
>
> It is quite natural to suppose that the Aryans brought this kind of warrior societies to South Asia from their northern homeland. However, on the Indian soil, the image of the dog/wolf as a symbol of battle fury and an emblem of a warriors' gang from the earliest times began to merge with the image of the more dangerous and widespread local predator—tiger/lion—and was later practically replaced by it.
> (Vassilkov forthcoming b)

The migrations of non-Vedic Aryans to the regions inhabited by either non-Aryan tribes or by a first pre-Vedic wave of Indo-Aryans would be a factor responsible for these analogies between the tribal societies of Deccan and South India and the most archaic culture of Indo-Aryans discovered by Günther-Dietz Sontheimer. The stanzas from Gaṅgādevī's poem leave no doubt that the mythological link between a hero (*vīra*) and a lion (*siṃha*) as well as the image of lion-warrior brotherhood was still very much alive in the minds of medieval poets.[190]

The hero of seven miniatures is Kamparāja himself. The brave king uses his sword (stanza 16) and javelin skilfully (stanza 18), and with his mace he hits the turbaned heads of the enemies (stanza 20).

na jāmadagnyena na rāghaveṇa
tathā na bhīmena na cārjunena /
āpāditas tena yathā samīke
harṣo maharṣeḥ kalahapriyasya // MV 9.22 //

Not even Praśurāma, Rāma, Bhīma or Arjuna
provided such joy to the sage,[191]
who was (always) fond of fights,
as he (Kampana) did in (this) battle.

But the most important moment in this battle is about to come—the combat with Tuluṣka. It seems that all the verses devoted to it have been preserved. Three stanzas (24, 25, 26) offer the description of this powerful enemy. The fight proper is presented in 11 stanzas. In two of them the author gives the picture of Kampana just before the moment of beheading the Sultan. It must be said that the figure of the Vijayanagara crown-prince with the magic sword in his raised hand and on his wonderful steed looks impressive. The goddess of Victory and Royal Prosperity definitely must have been standing by the side of such a hero:

---

[190] I am extremely grateful to Professor Yaroslav Vassilkov for allowing me not only to quote his paper delivered at the Indological Seminar "The broken world of sovereignty in India and beyond", University of Cagliari, Italy on 27th June 2013, but also for sending me two other articles of his: "The Mahābhārata and Non-Vedic Aryan Traditions" (forthcoming) and "Indian 'hero-stones' and the Earliest Anthropomorphic Stelae of the Bronze Age" published in: *Journal of Indo-European Studies*. Vol. 39, No. 1 & 2, Spring/Summer 2011.

[191] The divine sage Nārada is alluded to here. In Indian mythology he is a go-between who, because of his missions, is very often involved in conflicts and quarrels.

viṣacchaṭādhūmrarucir nṛpasya
karāgradhūtā karavālalekhā /
[jihveva reje]yavanādhirāja*
prāṇānilāñ jigrasiṣor bhujāheḥ // MV 9.36 //

The line of the sword in a dim colour of accumulated poison
was shining, shaken with the raised hand of the king.
It resembled the tongue of the snake
desiring to drink the lifebreath of the Yavana king.

sa vañcayaṃs tattaravāridhārāṃ
dhārāviśeṣapravaṇaupavāhyaḥ /
aśātayat tasya śiro nimeṣā—
[dane]na karṇāṭakulapradīpaḥ* // MV 9.37 //

Having the enduring horse,
he—the glory of the Karṇāṭa race—
avoiding the blade of his foe's sword,
cut off with it (his own sword) his (Sultan's) head in a moment.

Now we see a horrifying scene, but also showing an amazing courage of Kampana's opponent:

cyute 'pi śīrṣe caliṭāśvavalgā—
niyantraṇavyāpṛtavāmapāṇim /
pratiprahāraprasṛtānyahastaṃ
vīraḥ kabandhaṃ dviṣato 'bhyanandīt // MV 9.39 //

The hero (Kampana) saluted to his foe.
Even after his head had fallen,
the headless trunk holding the reins with the left hand
continued to restrain his speedy stallion
while the other hand stretched forth to give a counter-blow.

The canto ends with a conventional image showing the joy of gods—the flowers and auspicious rice was falling from the sky on Kampana's head. After the defeat of the Pārasikas, the region of the South shone like the river Yamuna deprived of the serpent,

Kāliya. In the very last stanza one more piece of information is added—Kampana guaranted safety to the rest of the defenders.

Summing up, Gaṅgādevī as the authoress of the *mahākāvya* and the singer of the glory of Vijayanagara, and in particular of Kampana, the crown-prince of the empire, implemented her task according to all the rules and requirements as far as the treatment of key issues, namely the battle(s) and victory(ies), is concerned. She devoted one 83-stanza-long chapter to Sambhuvarāya's victory and the concluding chapter to the victory over Madhurā Suratrāṇa. On the one hand, she, as the witness of these events, seems to provide the reader with precise data such as the names of rivers and places. On the other hand, the lack of interest in a more detailed and systematic description of the military operations is clearly visible. What really attracts the attention of the poetess is the figure of Kampana. Also here everything revolves around him. If he mounts his horse, it is this animal which receives as much attention as the decisive combat. Kampana is shown not only as the winner of both duels, but there are some other scenes showing his skills as a warrior. Perhaps in other historical *mahākāvya*s their heroes are not presented with such affection and dedication. Indeed, it is another proof that the author of this particular poem was emotionally close to the hero of the story and was not like one of the many court poets. Also the style of the passages devoted to the fights, besides conventional imagery, shows some traces peculiar to this particular court poem—the long passages devoted to one issue, such as the one dealing with the dust, or the recurrent subject of elephants' pearls. And the pictures combining the awful effects of war with 'delicate' matters, as in the comparison of sparks originated during the clash of weapons with glow-warms or the stronghold compared to the anthill (MV 4.77); finally, the two stanzas referring to pregnant women. It seems that the woman-writer's emotional attitudes and her point of view, despite all the limitations due to the literary conventions, are traceable in the poem.

Chapter 5
Intertextuality or Gaṅgādevī's Dialogue with Earlier *Kāvya* Poets

As already mentioned in this book, Gaṅgādevī's poem shows certain affinities with Kālidāsa's *Raghuvaṃśa* as far as the treatment of pregnancy and childbirth is concerned. Additionally, canto 8, with the mysterious woman appearing before Kampana, without any doubt is modelled on *Raghuvaṃśa* 16. The situation we are confronted with in both texts in the verses opening the respective *sargas* is exactly the same—both young kings seem to be unaware of the unstable condition on the territories under their reign and perfectly satisfied with their life of royal enjoyment. Kuśa does not realise that his misrule of the capital city, experiencing a period of total decline entailing a broken relationship with the goddess of royal fortune Śrī, can have detrimental effects on his rule and kingdom. Kampana, after conquering the Sambhuvarāyas, feels secure in his well-organised reality forgetting that just around the corner a foreign regime will replace the old order. The technique used by Kālidāsa while showing a picture of a dilapidated Ayodhyā is, to quote Tomasz Winiarski (forthcoming):

> (...) juxtaposing two images: one portraying the Indian reality—again, it is in fact *kāvya* "reality" but not devoid of elements of truth, such as the construction of the city, or better to say ideal

city, the portraits of ideal king and other members of society and their roles, etc.; the other image is purely fantastic. What we ought to add now is that they also contrast the two temporal planes: that of the past with this of the present. And once again Kālidāsa is using the literary technique which provokes a reader's cognitive dissonance: the frame of text's reality differs from what we expect. The image of present Ayodhyā existing in Kuśa's reality is totally unrealistic. The city is claimed by packs of jackal-like fantastic beasts *etc.* These descriptions of the mutilated and distorted reality are consistently interlaced by verses depicting bygone splendour of the same city. The latter realistic images are—paradoxically enough—referring to the non-existent state of reality which —(pun intended)—is no longer real.

Gaṅgādevī in her description of Śrīraṅgam and Madhurā also confronts the past with the present. But in the image of the present Tamil country, in place of fantastic beasts, she puts drunken Turks due to whom the old Brahmanical order has gone topsy-turvy. In this way she intensifies the message for the audience: Tuluṣkas behave like the demons or fantastic beasts, and Kampana, a son of Bukka I, is like Kuśa. If so, Bukka—his father—can be identified with Rāma—Kuśa's father. Kuśa was able to resolve the situation and revitalize both the capital city and his kingly power. Such is the destination of Kampana. This message was legible for all those who knew the *Raghuvaṃśa*, and there is no doubt that the educated recipient (*sahṛdaya*) was familiar with Kālidāsa's oeuvre. Such intertextual and intellectual plays were part and parcel of *kāvya* tradition, and Gaṅgā cleverly and consciously uses them.

To give more details concerning the similarities and dissimilarities between both passages, the poetess Gaṅgā and the master poet Kālidāsa present the king's way (in both cases the word *rājapatha* is used) as resounding with soft noise produced by the anklets worn by women (in RV 16.12 they are *abhisārikās* or women proceeding for a tryst; in the MV just charming women, mistresses—Skr. *ramaṇī*). The image of the horrifying present time is different: in the RV *rājapatha* is "now traversed by prey tracking she-jackals, which emit sparkles of fire from their growling muzzles";[192] in the MV 8 the tinkling of anklets is replaced with screams of Brahmanas being dragged in legs chains. The disturbance in performing rituals makes the divine women in both texts suffer (in both cases the verb *dūye* is used). Also here, in the *Madhurāvijaya*, the poor condition of the Tamil country is presented in connection with women,[193] although the way in which it affects their situation is completely different. As Richard Davis notices in his book *Lives of Indian Images* quoting the translation of the distich from the canto 8:

> "Its waters no longer restrained", reports the goddess, "the Kaveri River now overflows its ancient banks into all the wrong places, as if suddenly decided to imitate the Turks in following wicked pathways" (8.6). In this verse Gaṅgādevī suggests through double entendre that the young women of the area, like the flooding Kaveri, are transgressing the ancient codes of proper conduct and following the Turks into immoral pastimes. The new rulers pose a sexual threat.
> (Davies 1997: 117)

Most probably Gaṅgā's unnamed woman appears during the night, as happens in the *Raghuvaṃśa*. The beginning of the *sarga* is missing but the previous one contains the description of the evening and night, that is why one can suppose that the 'divine intervention' takes place during the night.

Obviously, Gaṅgādevī says a lot about ruined temples, and the final message formulated by the woman with the sword is different, but the presence of the literary intellectual game to which Gaṅgā invites her reader is the fact one cannot deny. One might also think that for a woman-writer it was tempting to show an episode in which a woman plays such an important role.

---

[192] Translation in Winiarski (forthcoming).

[193] For an exposition of the role of women in RV 16 see Winiarski (forthcoming).

There are also some parallels between the *Madhurāvijaya* and other works of *kāvya* masters. The case of *Vikramāṅkadevacaritam* of Bilhaṇa concerning the similarities between the exposition of the problems of poetics and the dialogue of the royal damsels has already been mentioned. One could also give the *Gītagovinda* of Jayadeva careful consideration as far as Gaṅgādevī's treatment of the spring season and the feelings of Kampana's wives and concubines toward their lover are concerned. Kampana's women can only think about their beloved. That is why they are drawing a picture of the king who, for them, is the god of love, just as in the case of Rādhā.

Jayadeva, *GG*, 4.8.5[194]

vilikhati rahasi kuraṅgamadena
bhavantam asamaśarabhūtam /
praṇamati makaram adho vinidhāya
kare ca śaraṃ navacūtam //

Being alone she draws you with the deer musk
in the shape of the god of love—
below she puts *makara* at your service,
in the hand she places the arrow of a fresh mango blossom.

In the *Madhurāvijaya* we read:

sutanavaḥ phalakeṣu madhūtsave
ratipatiṃ parilekhitum udyatāḥ /
hṛdayagocaratām aniśaṃ gataṃ
hariharātmajam eva samālikhan // MV 5.71 //

The beauties (of king's harem), during the spring festival,
commenced drawing Rati's husband (i.e. Kāma)
on the painting boards.

[194] Sandahl-Forgue 1977: 174.

Instead, they painted Kampana,[195]
incessantly present in the realm of their hearts.

The idea of painting a picture of the beloved as the god of love is the same in both stanzas although the images created differ in details. Anyway, the works of Kālidāsa, Jayadeva and Bilhaṇa must have been known to Gaṅgādevī as well as to her audience. Kālidāsa is honoured by the poetess in one of the very first stanzas of her poem. There is nothing about the *Gītagovinda* and *Vikramāṅkadevacarita*'s authors. The *Vikramāṅkadevacarita* originated in South India and treated about the history of the Cālukyas and the life and accomplishments of Vikramāditya Tribhuvanamalla of Kalyāṇa in particular. Definitely, it was the right composition to become an inspiration for someone who was also going to write a historical poem and promote the fame of the Sangamas, who just appeared on South Indian political stage. The *Gītagovinda* is one of the best known literary Indian texts, in South India included. Known as *Aṣṭapadī*, it is still performed

[195] Strangely enough, Kampana is introduced here as a son of Harihara—*hariharātmaja*. Perhaps we have to understand it as pointing to the fact that Bukka was a continuator of Sangama's line as well as his son Kampana. The compound word with *ātmaja* taken as "originating from intellect" (Monier-Williams 2005: 135) could be understood in a sense that Kampana was a "spiritual son" of Harihara. One could also think that Kampana is introduced here as an embodiment of Viṣṇu and Śiva, Hari-Hara. Such traits in the poem of Gaṅgādevī are present. The early Sangamas were Śaivas as is well known, Kampana, however, is shown as having among other auspicious marks on his body a Śrīvatsa mark on his breast, which clearly shows that he was supposed to be an *avatāra* of Viṣṇu. In fact, *purāṇic* and *dharmaśāstric* statements on kingship underline the fact that a king is an embodiment of Viṣṇu's royal power, i.e. a partial *avatāra* (*aṃśāvatāra*) of this god. Subrahmaṇyaśāstri's supposition that Harihara may have been another name for Kampana, and Gaurāmbikā another name for Devāyī (Subrahmaṇyaśāstrī 1969: B12) cannot be accepted. Harihara II, according to the inscriptions, was a son of Gaurāmbikā and he ruled after the death of his father in 1377. Kampana, a son of Devāyī, died before Bukka.

in the temples of South India or during *bhajana* congregational devotional worship.[196]

There is one more text which can be considered a potential source of Gaṅgā's inspiration, namely the work written by Bhaṭṭi (c. 7th c. A.D.) commonly known under the title *Bhaṭṭikāvya* (The Poem of Bhaṭṭi), bearing also other titles describing its contents, namely *Rāvaṇavadha*, *Rāmacarita* or *Rāmakāvya*. Bhaṭṭi describes the life of Rāma and simultaneously illustrates the rules of grammar and devices which belong to the realm of poetics. His poem belongs to the *mahākāvya* genre but at same time pertains to the *śāstrakāvya* type.

The distich of Gaṅgā showing the lotus-ised[197] rivers of blood at the battlefield reveals close affinity to the stanza composed by Bhaṭṭi.

Madhurāvijaya,
āsrāpagāsu parito nissṛtāsu sahasraśaḥ /
bhaṭānāṃ bhallanirlūnair ambhojāyitam ānanaiḥ //

Everywhere rushed forth thousands of rivers of blood,
lotus-ised with faces of warriors cut off by the *bhalla* arrows.

Bhaṭṭikāvya
saṃbabhūvuḥ kabandhāni prohuḥ śoṇitatoyagāḥ /
terur bhaṭāsyapadmāni dhvajaiḥ pheṇair ivābabhe //

Headless bodies gathered
and bloody water surged forward
in which soldiers' faces floated like lotuses
and banners looked like foam.[198]

---

196 More about *bhajanas* of South India in: Singer 1966 and Venkateswaran 1966.

197 This neologisms was for the first time used by David Smith while describing the place of lotus in the craft of *kāvya* poets (Smith 2000).

198 Translated by Lidia Szczepanik (Szczepanik 2010).

Chapter 14 of the *Bhaṭṭikāvya* describing the battle on Laṅkā is devoted to the presentation of the perfect tense system. This is the reason for introducing so many verbs. Gaṅgā was not bound by such tasks proper for *śāstrakāvya*, so there is no accumulation of verbs in her stanza; her aim, however, was the same—to create a shocking picture. As Lidia Szczepanik comments:

> The picture here is exceptionally gruesome when we realize that the image described is a grotesque distortion of the lotus pond theme so often used in *kāvya*. Originally, the lotus pond symbolises a tranquil beauty, it is often the meeting place of lovers but here, Bhaṭṭi seems to purposefully take this well-known theme and warp it into a ghastly scene that fills the reader with dread. Moreover, the face was so often compared to a lotus flower in Sanskrit poems that the comparison found here: the grimacing, cut-off faces of dead soldier floating in a river of blood, is entirely shocking.
> (Szczepanik 2010: 19)

Was Gaṅgādevī familiar with this bewildering Bhaṭṭi's proposal of employing the image of a pure lotus flower for battle scene description? Judging by the number of commentaries and authors quoting it, the *Bhaṭṭikāvya* was definitely well-known and popular in India and outside India, too.[199] Some verses from Bhaṭṭi's poem were included into the *kośa*s or the collections of most appreciated stanzas. Also Viśvanātha, mentioned by Gaṅgā in the first canto of her poem among the literati most venerated by her, refers to the *Bhaṭṭikāvya*.

The way of introducing evening and the moon-rising description reminds us that of the *Naiṣadhacarita*. Nala returns to Damayantī after performing evening rites and in the dialogue they describe to each other the moonshine and darkness. It might be that Gaṅgā was inspired by the beauty of this portion of Śrīharṣa's poem.

Gaṅgā speaks about poet Agastya, who authored seventy-four compositions. But only three works of this author have come

[199] More in: Sudyka 2004b: 25–28.

down to us: *Bālabhārata*, *Kṛṣṇacarita* and some fragments of *Nalakīrtikaumudi*. Possibly, this erudite poet and scholar had influenced the writings of our poetess as he belonged to the same region and was a maternal uncle of Viśvanātha, whom Gaṅgā named as a master shaping her scholarship. It is difficult to judge which of his works was the most liked and revered by Gaṅgādevī. It could be that the poetess was familiar with the concept of the caves treated as mouths emanating loud noise due to her studies of the *Kṛṣṇacarita*, where the Govardhana Mountain is compared to other mountains:

KC, *govardhanagirivarṇanam*, line 12–13[200]
(...) *mandaram apy apahasantam iva nirjaradhavanibhiḥ kandaramukhair* (...)

(it looked as though the Govardhana) laughed at the Mandara with its mouth-like caves echoing waterfalls.

In Gaṅgādevī's verse the mountain seems to yell out in fright "with its mouth-like caves resonating with the sounds of the wardrums": *taddundubhipratidhvānamukharaiḥ kandaramukhair* (MV 4.68).

Most probably a comparative study of preserved literary works of Agastya or Viśvanātha could reveal more such parallels and affinities. After all, studying the poems of the predecessors belonged to the education or *vyutpatti* of a poet. Drawing on the works written by the masters of Sanskrit literature and language could also show her expertise in the history of literature and of course 'speak' to the audience, allowing the connoisseurs (*sahṛdayas*) to taste and saviour the images evoked by other poets well-known to them but presented by Gaṅgādevī in a completely new attire. That was a skill expected on the part of a good poet—to bring associations with the most admired poets and literary

[200] Venkatacharya 1975: 39.

works. The 'creative' borrowings were part and parcel of the process of writing *kāvya* works. The poet could change the aesthetic emotion evoked by a certain image authored by his or her predecessor or link it to the new picture arising from his (or her) imagination, however, the path leading to the earlier work was traceable to the connoisseurs, who were proud whenever they could recognise familiar 'sounds' in a newly created composition. That was a kind of dialogue with past masters, too, but most importantly with the audience; establishing the basis for communication with sensitive listeners decoding a poem on the spot and reacting immediately to the familiar tunes. If we continue the comparison within the field of music, it was like developing the same motif for different musical instruments. Good execution of the motives, clear tunes and agreement with the rest of the composition could have brought the author a grand finale, the dream of each and every poet—fame and wealth. Exactly as Gaṅgādevī said:

karoti kīrtim arthāya kalpate hanti duṣkṛtam /
unmīlayati cāhlādaṃ kiṃ na sūte kaveḥ kṛtiḥ // MV 1.23 //

Is there anything the work of a poet does not yield?
It creates fame, brings wealth, destroys evil and gives delight.

Conclusions

The analysis of the epic poem *Madhurāvijaya* confirms the fact that it was authored by a woman. A considerable part of the composition is devoted to show the education of the poetess and her capability of writing according to the rules observed by Sanskrit *kāvya*. The world of arts was reserved almost exclusively for men, even if its patron is the goddess Sarasvatī. In the Sanskrit language, so rich in synonyms, there is no feminine form of the word *kavi* to denote a poetess. It may have made Gaṅgādevī very willing to prove her proper education: both in literary criticsm and history of literature. The suggestion that Viśvanātha could have been her teacher would be also a good move to show her own value as a poetess.[201] The fact that she was a talented pupil of Viśvanātha is attested by her poem[202]—an economy of words with a perfect choice of phrases that embody the emotional attitude of the author, an arrangement of sounds that attempt to achieve a maximum euphonic effect and an intelligent play with an implied reader.

It must also be said that the way in which the scenes from family life are presented and the attitude shown towards pregnancy, childbirth, family bonds and women at the court also demonstrate

---

[201] See the text and translation of the stanza devoted to Viśvanātha on p. 34.

[202] Even if the literary merits of the *Madhurāvijaya* have not been extensively discussed in the present monograph, its author hopes that the stanzas quoted here show the beauty of Gaṅgā's language and her deep knowledge of poet's profession.

a woman-writer's attitude. The interest in these particular subjects is clearly visible. Let us remember that a structure element of the political-military sequence important for the *mahākāvya*, namely a counsel, was replaced with a conversation between a father and his son. In this way, in the *Madhurāvijaya*, the dialogic parts indispensable for the *mahākāvya* are formed by causeries of harem ladies, a conversation between a prince and his court poetess, a talk between a father and his son and a speech of an unnamed woman—quite an unusual set of dialogues as for the *mahākāvya*, the aim of which is to present a victory, not employed by other *mahākāvya* creators of *vijaya*-type *mahākāvyas*. Also the stylistics of the work shows certain preferences of its creator. In particular, the figure of the king receives a lot of attention. As we already know, he was described in detail first as a newborn child, then a youth, a married man among his women and finally as a great warrior. In fact, the pictures of the battles are created to provide the scenery in which he is presented. And all these pictures of Kampana speak about close and affectionate bonds of the author of such a presentation with the person depicted.

It could also be stated that the pictures from a woman's life at the king's court are more visible and more vivid in the *Madhurāvijaya* than in any other male-authored works. No wonder, the authoress of the poem knew life in the king's harem very well. These pictures are satiated with colours which usually fade in conventional delineation of a king's life as presented by male literati. We see women at the court in their different roles—as a mother, wife, lover, dancer, musician, poet, maidservant and a chowri bearer while an audience was being granted to other kings. The women's world naturally revolves around one man. The scenes in the harem we are witnessing are in accordance with convention (*kavisamaya*), but the poetess always throws more light on this very little known sphere of court's life. The king's and his ladies' frolicking in water (*jalakrīḍā, jalakeli*) is depicted in canto 6 in a very conventional way but the description of the walk to the pleasure lake and the conversation we can overhear allows us to visualise this moment in the everyday life of the harem, especially with the closing scene—Kampana watches his women as they change into fresh clothes and tie their hair. However, the time for entertainment has come to an end:

tataḥ sairandhrībhiḥ kṛtasamucitākalparacanaḥ
purandhrībhiḥ sārdhaṃ samadhigataśuddhāntavasatiḥ /
trayīgītaṃ tejas tripuraharam ārādhya vidhivad
yathārhair vyāpārair narapatir ahaḥśeṣam anyat // MV 6.69 //

Then the king, suitably attired by the dress-maidens,
entered the inner quarters with the eldest matrons.
There he worshipped,
in accordance with *śāstra*,
the divine light to whom the triple *Vedas* pay tribute,
the tormentor of Tripura[203],
and spent the rest of the day in fitting occupations.[204]

Such an introduction and end to the *jalakrīḍā* makes the picture realistic. This time frolicking in water is not just one of the elements ornamenting the *mahākāvya* genre and recommended by theoreticians. The whole 69-stanza-long *sarga* is created around this motif and in such a way that the audience could treat this chapter as a kind of report presenting a few hours from normal court life.

As to the historical value of the *Madhurāvijaya*, it should be stressed that it is not a historical document in the strict sense but one of narrative "histories" written by Indian court poets. In the colophons closing each canto the word *carita* appears:

iti śrīgaṅgādevyā viracite madhurāvijayanāmni
vīrakamparāyacarite prathamaḥ sargaḥ /

---

[203] Śiva.

[204] Transl. Rajaraman & Kotamraju 2013: 73.

> This is the first [and similarly: second, third, etc.] canto in the life-story of Kamparāya, entitled the Conquest of Madhurā.

As a term pertaining to genology, it refers to a biography, i.e. the genre recording significant events in the life of a historical person. However, also in Western culture, what a biographer usually does is to interpret and explain certain facts as well as present a character in a lively, interesting and also entertaining manner. If so, a biography, besides its historical aspects, portrays artistic and fictitious characters, too. Ronald Steiner, in his article "Truth under the Guise of Poetry. Aśvaghoṣa's *Life of the Buddha*", notices this twofold nature of biographies. He writes that on the one side there is "the lived life of a certain person" and on the other, "'same' life imagined or conceived by an author".[205] There was no need for Gaṅgādevī to imagine the life of her hero, as she was witnessing it day by day. Her task, however, was to allow some other people to imagine it, but in a proper way. This "proper way" was customized first of all to fit Vijayanagara politics, to meet an implied reader's expectations and conform to the rules prescribed for *kāvya*. Among implied readers was Kampana himself and his court, as well as King Bukka I, and perhaps other Vijayanagara-influenced/dependent courts.

The *Madhurāvijaya* usefulness for studying medieval South India cannot be questioned; nevertheless, a broad, contextual reading of such an indigenous source is required as well as its comparison with other texts and epigraphical records, if there are any, addressing the same episodes. One should bear in mind that:

> Before asking how these texts may (or may not) accurately reflect that past, we must first attempt to understand the particular forms and contents of their representation according to their own cultural logic.
> (Wagoner 2000: 304)

[205] Steiner 2010: 90.

Trivialising Wagoner's statement and focusing on our texts creating different historical personages to become victors over *suratrāṇa*, we could say that actually it is not so important who exactly killed the Muslim ruler but how and for what purpose the Madhurā triumph was used and in what circles announced.

If the real conqueror of the Sultan was Sāluva Maṅgi, he still was a general of Kampana, and his success and that of Kampana's troops could be ascribed in a very natural manner to Kampana himself. Again, Kampana was a son of Bukka I and was acting in his name; so following the same line of thought the victory was also his father's. In that case, Gaṅgādevī, in her poem, the presentation of which could be restricted in fact only to the court of Kampana, could show her beloved as a hero of the battle in a symbolic sense. It is certain that he fought many battles for Vijayanagara and won many times. In some royal inscriptions, it was Bukka I who was the winner of the combat, as this time the discourse about "what happened" was on a state level and the role of inscriptional *praśasti*s was to proclaim and establish the glory of the dynasty and kingdom through the deeds of its ruler.

If we deny Sāluva's role as a victor, the versions presented in both *mahākāvya*s, the *Rāmābhyudaya* and *Sāluvābhyudaya*, have to be treated as a part of the foundation legend of the Sāluvas, explaining why their line deserved the Vijayanagara throne. The message for the courtiers and the subjects was clear—because of the merits of their ancestors and the will of the gods.

Taking into account the presupposition that Gaṅgā's poem was like her "nocturnal poem" closing canto 7, a work of the scope limited to Kampana's court only, the question arises: how could it survive until the present day? If we think about the *Madhurāvijaya* as one of the early texts reacting against the order introduced by the newcomers to the region, it gains importance as it inscribes into a class of culturally and politically important works described as the epics of resistance (Aziz Ahmad's term introduced in his article "Epic and Counter-epic in Medieval India") or the epics of reconquest (Richard H. Davis' term proposed in the third and fourth chapter of his book *Lives of Indian Images*). As such it belonged to indigenous historiographic discourse about the past. Some passages of the *Madhurāvijaya* could even sharpen the "communally inspired image of Vijayanagara as a Hindu state, dedicated to the containment of Islam and the preservation of the traditional Hindu cultural order in the south" (Wagoner 2000: 301). However, in recent years, the understanding of the transcultural processes in medieval India has been deepened and various Vijayanagara-oriented projects have brought to light new facts or made possible their different interpretations, a fact that also helps evaluate Gaṅgādevī's work and appreciate its significance as a Vijayanagara-period narrative. It is also worth pointing out that this poem shows the great poetic skills of its author.[206] Listening to such poetry could really have been as enjoyable in the past as it is now.

[206] In the introductory part to the *Madurāvijaya* edition of Subrahmaṇyaśāstrī, Kasi Krishnamacharya, a poet himself, presents such an opinion: "It might sound blasphemous to say that the poetess Gangadevi excelled divine Kalidasa in flight of poetic imagination and yet it appears to be true" (Subrahmaṇyaśāstrī 1969: B 46).

Postscriptum or What Happened to our Heroes after the Conquest of Madhurā

We do not know if the canto describing the battle with the Sultan was really the last one. In fact, the aim announced by the poetess in the title of her poem, namely *vijaya*, had been achieved—the Sultan was defeated. Anyway, one could expect a closing chapter describing the restoration of normal life after the Muslim occupation and the further prosperous rule of Kampana. As we are left without any information in the *mahākāvya* about the period following the victorious battle, we can turn to inscriptions only to satisfy our curiosity as to the fortunes of Kampa and Gaṅgā. It seems that the Tamil country was well administered by him, perhaps with the help of his son Jammaṇa or Jommaṇṇa, whose name appears in inscriptions from the Gingee area.[207] In 1374 Bukka I visited (inspected?) his viceroyalty, as is attested by an epigraph (Srinivasan 1990: 85). In the same year, the victor in the battle with the Sultan of Madhurā died.[208] The last in-

[207] The inscription from Eyil in Gingee taluk, dated 1369, is perhaps the earliest among those referring to Jammaṇa (Srinivasan 1990: 85).

[208] Subrahmaṇyaśāstrī, in his historical introduction to his edition of the *Madhurāvijaya*, claimed that it was not Vīra Kampana, the Madhurā victor, who died in 1374. As we know his younger brother and uncle also bore this name. According to Subrahmaṇyaśāstrī, Kampana had another name and ruled as

scription mentioning his name, dated 2nd October 1374, is from Tirupullāṇi. In the inscription from Tiruvannamalai, dated 17th December 1374, Jammaṇa introduces himself as a ruler of the earth, Kampana's son, who was a son of Bukka, and offers some land to the Aruṇacaleśvara temple for chanting the Vedas "by one person daily till the moon and the sun endure" as a part of rites following his father Kampana's death.[209] It is highly probable that it was a part of a purification ceremony which takes place one month after death. If so, it would mean that Kampana must have died in mid-November, 1374. His father, Bukka I, outlived him, dying in 1377.

One can speculate on Kampana's age at the moment of his death, believing Gaṅgādevī's words that he was a very young

---

Harihara II after the death of Bukka. The inscriptional eulogies served the learned editor and commentator as proof. He cites the inscription at Vijayanagara of 1382: "With the conquest of Chola, Pandya, and Kerala regions, his repute was reflected as in a mirror in the entire South India. Though he always set out for invasion in Sarat (...) the sky would be always cloudy with the tears of the wives of the Muslims he killed" (Subrahmaṇyaśāstrī 1969: B26). Even if such words bring to mind Kampana's southern campaign, there is no direct statement in this particular inscription and some others that Harihara was a conqueror of Madhurā and the mentions of commencing the military expedition in autumn and tears of enemies' wives accord with rhetoric used in the epic poems as well as in the *praśastis*. It is visible that Subrahmaṇyaśāstrī treats the *Madhurāvijaya* of Gaṅgādevī as a regular chronicle in which the author relates events systematically and in accordance with historical truth. However, it is a poem which the poetess wrote in order to show in nice words and pictures the glory of Kampana and splendour of the Sangama dynasty and kingdom. Additionally, it would be also possible to point out inscriptions which create quite a different picture. For instance, the inscription on a stone set up at Modalli, Kollegal Taluk corresponding to 1392 (A.R. No. 247 of 1913.) informs that in the reign of Harihara the fields and houses once granted by Hiriya Kampana to Brahmanas of Modehalli named Kamparājapura were restored to them. Judging by this inscription King Harihara and Hiriya Kampana were two different persons.

[209] The text and the translation of this inscription can be found in Srinivasan 1990: 422–423.

prince—just after finishing his education and then getting married—when he was sent by his father for his *digvijaya* around 1351. If it is true, Kampana must have been in his early or middle forties when he died. As we know his son Jammaṇa was his successor, but it seems that he did not stay long in Tamil country. As Srinivasan mentions:

> Subsequently, in A.D. 1375 he was rulling in east Mysore (*E.C.*, X Ct. 94). It indicates his transfer from Tamiḻnāṭu to Mysore. After this date Jammaṇa is not heard of. What happened to this prince later on is not known.
> (Srinivasan 1990: 85)

The epigraphical evidence is silent about women from Kampana's family. We do not know what Gaṅgādevī's lot was. What is now obvious is the fact that her poem must have been written before 1374, and so perhaps she commenced its writing immediately after Kampana's triumph to commemorate the deeds of the victor in the battle of Madhurā "till the moon and the sun shine".

Appendix
The Subject Matter of the *Madhurāvijaya*

Chapter 1: Praise of the literary predecessors of Gaṅgādevī and her poetic manifesto. The description of the Vijayanagara city and King Bukka I.

Chapter 2: Devāyī gives birth to her first son; the childhood of Prince Kampana.

Chapter 3: Prince Kampana's description. King Bukka instructs his son Kampana.

Chapter 4: March of Kampana's army and the battle with Sambhuvarāya.

Chapter 5: Kampana's just rule in Tuṇḍīramaṇḍalam. The King's lovemaking throughout all the seasons of the year.

Chapter 6: The King and his ladies frolicking in the water.

Chapter 7: Description of sunset, moon-rising and night.

Chapter 8: The speech of a mysterious woman depicting the Tamil country under Muslim rule.

Concluding canto: The battle with the Sultan.

List of Illustrations

Figures

Tables

Abbreviations and Bibliography

Primary sources and/or their translations

AS = ***Abhītistava*** of Vedānta Deśika

Ramaswamy Ayyangar, D. 1987. *Abheeti-Stavam by Vedanta Desika. With Meaning and Commentary in English by D. Ramaswamy Ayyangar.* Madras: Visishtadvaita Pracharini Shabha.

Acyutarāyābhyudaya of Rājanātha III Ḍiṇḍima

1. Krishnamachariar, R. V. (ed. & com.). 1907. *Achyutaraya Abhyudayam.* No. 6. Srirangam: Sri Vani Vilas Press.
2. Krishna Aiyangar, A. N. (ed.). 1945. *Acyutarāyābhudaya of Rājanātha III Ḍiṇḍima (Sargas 7 to 12).* Madras: Adyar Library.

AŚ = ***Arthaśāstra*** of Kauṭilīya

1. Jolly, J. and R. Schmidt (eds.). 1923. *Arthaśāstra of Kauṭilya. A New Edition.* Lahore: Motilal Banarsidas.
2. Kangle, R. P. (ed.). 2010 (2nd edition. Reprint). *The Kauṭilīya Arthaśāstra. Part I. Sanskrit Text with a Glossary.* Delhi: Motilal Banarsidass.
3. Kangle, R. P. (transl.). 2000 (2nd edition. Reprint). *The Kauṭilīya Arthaśāstra. Part II. An English Translation with Critical and Explanatory Notes.* Delhi: Motilal Banarsidass.

Bālabhārata of Agastya Paṇḍita

Ramamurthy, K. S. 1983. *Balabharatam of Agastya Pandita.* Tirupati: Sri Venkateswara University, Oriental Research Institute.

Bhaṭṭikāvya of Bhaṭṭi

Trivedi, K. P. 1898. *Bhaṭṭi-Kāvya or Rāvaṇavadha* composed *by Śri Bhaṭṭi ed. with the commentary of Mallinātha and with critical and explanatory notes by K. P.Trivedî.* 2 vols. Bombay Sanskrit Series no. 56. Bombay.

Cola Campū of Virūpākṣa

Raghavan, V. (ed.). 1951. *Cola Campū of Virūpākṣa. Edited with Critical Introduction and Notes.* Tanjore Saraswati Mahal Series. No. 55. Madras.

Gītagovinda of Jayadeva

1. Stoler Miller, B. (ed. and transl.). 1984. *The Gītagovinda of Jayadeva. Love Song of the Dark Lord.* Delhi: Motilal Banarsidass.
2. Sandahl-Forgue, S. 1977. *Le Gītgovinda. Tradition et innovation dans le kāvya.* Louvain: Sandahl-Forgue.

HC = ***Harṣacarita*** of Bāṇa

Kane, P. V. (ed.). 1965. *The Harshacarita of Bāṇabhaṭṭa with Exhaustive Notes [Ucchvāsas I-VIII].* Delhi: Motilal Banarsidass.

Kādambarī of Bāṇabhatta

Parab, Kāśīnāth Pāṇḍurang (ed.). 1908. *The Kādambarī of Bāṇabhatta and his son Bhūshaṇabhatta. With the Commentaries of Bhānuchandra and his Disciple Siddhachandra (Proteges of the Emperor Akbar), edited by Kāśīnāth Pāṇḍurang Parab.* Bombay: Tukārām Jāvajī, Nirṇaya-Sāgar Press.

KS = *Kāmasūtra*

Gosvami, D. L. (ed.). 1912. *Kāmasūtram. Vātsyāyanamunipraṇītaṃ. Pūrṇayā Jayamaṅgalaracitayā ṭīkayā sametam.* Benares: Chowkhamba Sanskrit Book Depot.

Kathāsaritsāgara of Somadeva

1. Śāstri, J. L. (ed.) 1970. *Kathāsaritsāgara.* Delhi–Patna–Varanasi: Motilal Banarsidass.
2. Tawney, C. H. (transl.). 1880. *The Kathāsaritsāgara or Ocean of the Streams of Story.* Calcutta.

KA–Bh. = *Kāvyālaṅkāra* of Bhāmaha

1. Śarma, B. N. and B. Upādhyāya (eds.). 1928. *Kāvyālaṅkāra of Bhāmaha.* Kashi Sanskrit Series, 61. Varanasi.
2. Naganatha Sastry, P. V. (ed.). 1991 (reprint). *Kāvyālaṅkāra of Bhāmaha. Edited with English Translation and Notes.* Delhi: Motilal Banarsidass.

KA–D. = *Kāvyādarśa* of Daṇḍin

1. Shastri, V. (ed.). 1938. *Kāvyādarśa of Daṇḍin. Edited with an Original Commentary by Vidyābhhūṣaṇa Pandit Rangacharya Raddi Shastri.* Government Oriental Series–Class A. No. 4. Poona: Bhandarkar Oriental Institute.
2. Panda R. K. (ed.). 2008 (Revised Edition). *Kāvyādarśa* of Daṇḍin. *Text with the Commentary of Jibānand Vidyāsāgar. Translation in English by V.V. Sastrulu.* Delhi: Bharatiya Kala Prakashan.
3. Dimitrov, D. (ed.). 2002. *Mārgavibhāga. Die Unterscheidung der Stilarten, Kritische Ausgabe des ersten Kapitels von Daṇḍin Poetik Kāvyādarśa und der tibetischen Űbertragung Sñan ṅag me loṅ nebst einer deutschen Űbersetzung des Sanskrittextes, Herausgegeben nach nepalesischen Handschriften des Sanskrit-*

textes und der kanonischen und ausserkanonischen tibetischen Űberlieferung unter besonderer Berücksichtigung der älteren Kommentarliteratur, sammt Glossaren, ausfürlichen Bibliographien, Konkordanzen und Indizes. Marburg: Indica et Tibetica Verlag.

KA = *Kirātārjunīya* of Bhāravi

1. Kale, M. R. (ed. and transl.). 1998 (First ed. 1966). *The Kirātārjunīya of Bhāravi, Cantos I – III, Text with Mallinātha's Commentary, Prose Order of the Ślokas, Notes, Translations into English and Hindi M. R. Kale.* Delhi: Motilal Banarsidass.
2. Durgaprasad & K. Pandurang Parab. (ed.). 1902. *The Kirātārjunīya of Bhāravi with the commentary (Ghaṇṭāpatha) of Mallinātha and various readings ed. by Mahāmahopādhyaya Paṇdit Durgāprasāda and Kāśīnātha Pāṇḍuraṅga Paraba.* Bombay: Tukaram.

Krīḍâbhirāmamu by Vinukŏṇḍa Vallabharāya

Rao, V. N. and D. Shulman (transl.). 2002. *A lover's guide to Warangal: The Krīḍâbhirāmamu by Vinukŏṇḍa Vallabharāya. Transl. [from the Telugu] by Velcheru Narayana Rao and David Shulman & with a afterword by Phillip B. Wagoner.* Delhi: Permanent Black.

KC = Kṛṣṇacarita of Agastyapaṇḍita

Venkatacharya, T. 1975. The *Kṛṣṇacarita of Agastyapaṇḍita (A Gadyakāvya). Edited with Introduction and Notes in English.* Tanjore Sarasvati Mahal Series vol. 155. Thanjavur: Tanjore Maharaja Serfoji's Sarasvati Mahal Library.

Kṛṣṇakarṇāmṛta of Līlāśuka Bilvamaṅgala

Wilson, F. (ed.). 1975. *The Love of Krishna, The Kṛṣṇakarṇāmṛta of Līlāśuka Bilvamaṅgala.* Philadelphia: University of Pennsylvania Press.

Livro em que dá relação do que viu e ouviu no Oriente of Duarte Barbosa.

Dames, M. L. 1918, 1921. *The book of Duarte Barbosa: An Account of the Countries Bordering on the Indian Ocean and their Inhabitants. Written by Duarte Barbosa and completed about the year 1518 A.D.* Vol. I-II. London: Hakluyt Society.

MV = ***Madhurāvijaya*** of Gaṅgādevī

1. Miśra, Ś. (ed.). 2001. *Madhurāvijaya-mahākāvyam.* Patna: Śrī Śāradā Publications.
2. Rajaraman, S. & V. Kotamraju (transl.). 2013. *The Conquest of Madhurā by Gaṅgādevī.* Bangalore: Rasāla.
3. Sastri, Harihara G. and S. Sastri (eds.). 1924. *Madhura Vijaya or Virakamparaya Charita. An Historical Kavya by Ganga Devi.* Trivandrum: The Sridhara Power Press.
4. Subrahmaṇyaśāstrī, P. (ed.). 1969. Madhurāvijayam. Tenali.
5. Thiruvenkatachari, S. (ed.). 1957. *Madhurāvijaya of Gangā Devi.* Annamalainagar: Annamalai University.

MBh = ***Mahābhārata***

Mahābhārata. 1971. 4 vols. Poona: Bhandarkar Oriental Research Institute.

Pāṇḍyakulodaya of Maṇḍalakavi

Sarma, K. V. 1981. *Pāṇḍyakulodaya (Resurgence of the Pāṇḍya Race). A Historical Mahākāvya by Maṇḍalakavi. Critically Edited with Introduction, Translation and Appendices.* Hoshiarpur: Punjab University Indological Series 27.

Raghunāthābhyudaya of Rāmabhadrāmbā

Chintamani, T. R. (ed.). 1934. *Raghunāthābhyudaya of Rāmabhadrāmbā. [A Historical Poem].* University of Madras. Madras: Ananda Press.

RV = ***Raghuvaṃśa*** of Kālidāsa

Kale, M. R. (ed.). 1972 (reprint).*The* ***Raghuvaṃśa*** *of Kālidāsa with the Commentary Sañjīvanī of Mallinātha, cantos I–V, ed. with a literal English translation and copious notes by M. R. Kale.* Delhi–Varanasi–Patna: Motilal Banarsidass.

RA = ***Rāmābhyudaya*** of Aruṇagirinātha Ḍiṇḍima (ascribed to Sāluva Narasiṃha)

Visalakshy, P. (ed.). 2003. *Rāmābhyudayam.* Trivandrum Sanskrit Series 267. Thiruvananthapuram: SB Press (P) Limited.

SA = *Sāluvābhyudaya* of Rājanātha III Ḍiṇḍima

Sāluvābhyudaya—manuscript DC No. 11818 & 11819, Govt. Oriental MSS Library, Chennai.

SR = ***Samdeśarāsaka*** of Abdul Rahman

1. Jina Vijaya Muni and Harivallabh Bhayani (eds. and transl.). 1945. *Samdeśarāsaka: (a unique work of a Muslim poet in Apabhramsa language), Abdul Rahaman.* Singhi Jain Series 22. Bombay.
2. Mayerhofer, C. M. 1998. *The Samdeśarāsaka of Abdul Rahman.* Delhi: Motilal Banarsidass Publishers.

Saugandhikāharaṇa of Viśvanāthakavi

Śivadatta and Kasinath Pandurang. 1902. *The Saugandhikâharaṇa of Vizvanâthakavi. Kâvymâlâ 74.* Bombay: 'Nirnaya-Sagara' Press.

Śrīrāmāyaṇasāra Kāvya Tilakam by Madhuravāṇī

Ramaraju, B. (ed.). 1971. *Śrīrāmāyaṇasāra Kāvya Tilakam by Madhuravāṇī.* Andhrapredesh Sahitya Akademi. Hydarabad: Dakshina Bharat Press.

Śṛṅgāramañjarī by Akbar Shah

Raghavan, V. (ed.). 1951. *Sringaramanjari of Saint Akbar Shah. Based on old Sanskrit Manuscripts in Devanagari and Telugu Scripts. Edited with a Critical Study by V. Raghavan.* Hyderabad : Hyderabad Government, Archaeological Department.

ŚŚ = *Śyainika Śāstra* of Rājā Rudradeva

Shastri, H. (ed. and transl.). 1910. *Śyainika Śāstra or a Book on Hawking by Rājā Rudradeva of Kumaon.* Calcutta: Asiatic Society.

VPC = ***Varadāmbikā Pariṇaya Campū*** of Tirumalāmbā

Suryakanta (ed.). 1970. *Varadāmbikā Pariṇaya Campū of Tirumalāmbā. With English Translation, Notes & Introduction.* Varanasi: Chowkhambha Sanskrit Series Office.

VC = ***Vikramāṅkadevacaritam*** of Bilhaṇa

1. Banerji, S. C. and A. K. Gupta (eds.). 1968. *Bilhaṇa's Vikramāṅkadeva Caritam. Glimpses of the History of Cālukyas of Kalyāṇa. First English rendering.* Calcutta: Sambodhi Publications.
2. Bühler, G. (ed.). 1875. *The Vikramânkadevacharita. A Life of King Vikramâditya-Tribhuvanamalla of Kalyâṇa. Composed by Vidyâpati Bilhaṇa.* Bombay Sanskrit Series Vol. XIV. Bombay: Gomernment Central Book Depot.

VdhP = ***Viṣṇudharmottara-purāṇa***

Shah, P. (ed.). 1958. *Viṣṇudharmottara-purāṇa Third Khaṇḍa.* (Vol.1: Text, Critical Notes etc.). Baroda: Baroda Oriental Institute.

Inscriptions

EI = Chakravarti N. P. (ed.). 1942. *Epigraphia Indica and Record of Archaeological Survey of India.* Vol. XXIV. 1937-1938. Calcutta: Government of India Press.

Filliozat, V. 1973. *L'Épigraphie de Vijayanagar du début?* 1377. Paris: École Française D'Extrême-Orient.

Gopal, B. R. and S. Ritti (eds). 2004. *The Inscriptions of the Vijayanagara Rulers.* Vol. I, II, III. New Delhi: Indian Council of Historical Research.

Rangacharya, M. and S. Kuppuswami Sastri. 1918. *A Triennial Catalogue of Manuscripts 1910–11 to 1912–13 for the Governmental Oriental Manuscript Library Madras.* Vol. IV, Part. I, Part III. Madras: Government Press.

EC = Rice, B. L. 1905. *Epigraphia Carnatica.* Vol. X. *Inscriptions in the Kolar District.* Mangalore: Basel Mission Press.

Sastri, Kuppuswami S. 1917. *A Triennial Catalogue of Manuscripts.* Vol. II, Part I. Madras: Government Press.

Sastry Shama R. and N. Lakshminarayan Rao (eds.). *Kannada Inscriptions from the Madras Presidency.* Vol. IX. Online access: `http://www.whatisindia.com/inscriptions/south_indian_inscriptions/volume_9/vijayanagara_548.html`/5th Febraury 2013.

Srinivas, P. R. (ed.). 1990. *Tiruvannamalai, a Śaiva sacred complex of South India. Inscriptions.* Vol. 1. Part 1, Part 2. Introduction, edition, translation P.R. Srinivas; Indexes, topography Marie-Louise Reiniche. Pondicherry: Institute français de Pondicherry.

Vijayaraghavacharya, V. (Ed. & Transl.). 1984 (Second Ed.). *Inscriptions of Achyutaraya's Time: From 1530 A.D. to 1542 A.D.* Delhi: Sri Satguru Publications.

Secondary literature

Ahmad, A. 1963. Epic and Counter-epic in Medieval India. *Journal of the American Oriental Society* 83. No. 4: 470–476.

Aiyangar, Krishnaswamy S. (ed.). 2003 (First ed. 1919). *Sources of Vijayanagara History. Selected and edited by S. Krishnaswami Aiyangar.* New Delhi: Aryan Books International.

Ali, D. 2000. Royal Eulogy as World History: Rethinking Copper-plate Inscriptions in Cōḷa India. In: R. Inden, J. Walters, D. Ali (ed.). *Querying the Medieval: Texts and the History of Practices in South Asia.* Oxford etc.: Oxford University Press: 165–229.

—. 2004. *Courtly culture and political life in early medieval India.* Cambridge Studies in Indian History and Society 10. Cambridge: Cambridge University Press.

Asher, C. B. and C. Talbot. 2006. *India before Europe.* Cambridge: Cambridge University Press.

Babu, Sridhara D. 1975. *Kingship: state and religion in South India according to South Indian historical biographies of kings (Madhurāvijaya, Acyutarāyābhudaya and Vemabbhūpalacarita).* Ph.D. Dissertation. Göttingen.

Bhatta, Panduranga C. 1997. *Contribution of Karnāṭaka to Sanskrit.* Chennai: Institute of Asian Studies.

Bronner, Y. 2010. The Poetics of Ambivalence: Imagining and Unimagining the Political in Bilhaṇa's Vikramāṅkadevacarita.

In: Journal of Indian Philosophy (2010) 38: 457–483 DOI 10.1007/s10781-010-9100-1

—. (forthcoming). *Birds of a Feather: Vāmana Bhaṭṭa Bāṇa's Haṃsasandeśa and its Intertexts.* In: Journal of the American Oriental Society 133.3 (2013).

Chaudhari, J. B. 2001 (First published 1939–1943). *The Contribution of Women to Sanskrit Literature. Vol.* 1–3. Delhi: Cosmo Publications.

Dallapiccola, A. L. 1998. *Sculpture at Vijayanagara. Iconography and Style. Manohar-New Delhi: American Institute of Indian Studies.*

Davis, R. H. 1993. Indian Art Objects as Loot. *Journal of Asian Studies* 52. No. 1: 22–48.

—. 1997. *Lives of Indian Images.* Princeton-New Jersey: Princeton University Press.

Deshpande, C. R. 1992. *Studies in Campū Literature.* Delhi-Varanasi: Bharatiya Vidya Prakashan.

Dodamani, B. A. 2008. *Gaṅgādevī's Madhurāvijayam. A literary Study.* Delhi: Sharada Publishing House.

Durga Prasad, J. 1988. *History of the Andhras upto 1565 A.D.* Guntur: PG Publishers.

Eaton, R. M. 2000. Temple Desecration and Indo–Muslim States. In: R. M. Eaton (ed.). *Essays on Islam and Indian History.* New Delhi: Oxford University Press: 94–132. First published in: D. Gilmartin and B. B. Lawrence. 2000. *Beyond Turk and Hindu: Rethinking Religious Identities in Islamicate South Asia.* Gainesville: University Press of Florida: 246–281.

Elliot, H. M. and J. Dowson. 1966 (reprint. First published 1867–77. London: Trübner and Co.). *The History of India as Told by its Own Historians: Muhammadan Period.* 8 vols. New York: AMS Press.

Emeneau, M. B. 1985. Kannaḍa Kampa, Tamil Kampaṉ: Two Proper Names. In: *Journal of the American Oriental Society*. Vol. 105, No. 3. Indological Studies Dedicated to Daniel H. H. Ingalls (Jul.–Sep., 1985): 401–404.

Fuller, C. J. 2007 (First ed. 1984). *Servants of the Goddess. The Priests of a South Indian Temple*. Cambridge etc.: Cambridge University Press.

Galewicz, C. 2009. *A Commentator in Service of the Empire. Sāyaṇa and the Royal Project of Commenting on the Whole of the Veda*. Publications of the De Nobili Research Library. Edited by Gerhard Oberhammer, Utz Podzeit & Karen Preisendanz. Vol. 35. Wien.

Gopala Rao, A. 1969. *Lepakshi*. Hyderabad: The Andhra Pradesh Lalit Kala Akademi.

Hardy, P. 1997 (reprint. First published 1960. London: Luzac and Company Ltd.). *Historians of Medieval India: Studies in Indo–Muslim Historical Writing*. New Delhi: Munshiram Manoharlal.

Heras, H. 1929. *Beginnings of Vijayanagara History*. Bombay: Indian Historical Research Institute.

Hiebert, H. J. 1985. Sanskrit poetry by three Vijayanagara queens. In: A. L. Dallapiccola and S. Zingel-Avé Lallemant (eds.). *Vijayanagara—City and Empire. New Currents of Research*. Stuttgart: Steiner Verlag Wiesbaden GMBH: 97–100.

—. 1989. Tradition and innovation in Sanskrit Mahākāvya: The Harem sunset. In: A. L.Dallapiccola (ed.). *Shastric Traditions in Indian Arts*. Stuttgart: Steiner: 269–283.

Hodgson, M. G. S. 1974. *The venture of Islam: Conscience and History in World Civilization*. Vol. 1. Chicago–London: University of Chicago Press.

Hodivala, Shahpurshah H. 1979 (First published: Vol. 1 1939; Vol. 2 1957). *Studies in Indo–Muslim History: A Critical*

Commentary on Elliot and Dowson's History of India as told by its own historians. 2 vols. Lahore: Islamic Book Service.

Jackson, W. J. 2005. *Vijayanagara Voices. Exploring South Indian History and Hindu Literature*. Hampshire: Ashgate.

Kameswara Rao, V. 1982. *The Lepakshi Temple*. Tirupati: T. V. Press.

Kanaka Durga, P. S. and Y. A. Sudhakar Reddy. 1992. Kings, Temples and Legitimation of Autochthonous Communities. A Case Study of a South Indian Temple. In: *Journal of the Economic and Social History of the Orient*. Vol. 35, No. 2. Brill: 145–166.

Karashima, N. 1993. *Towards a new formation: South Indian society under Vijayanagar rule*. Delhi: Oxford University Press.

—. 2001. Whispering of Inscriptions. In: K. R. Hall (ed.). *Structure and Society in early South India. Essays in Honour of Noboru Karashima*. Oxford University Press.

Katragadda, S. L. 1996. *Women in Vijayanagara. Women in 16th Century (A Study of Tuluva Dynasty)*. Delhi-Hyderabad-Bangalore-Madras: Delta Publishing House.

Kaul, Sh. 2010. *Imagining the Urban. Sanskrit and the City in Early India*. Delhi: Permanent Black.

Kotraiah, C. T. M. 2003. *King, Court and Capital. An Anthology of Kannada Literary Sources from Vijayanagara Period*. New Delhi: Manohar, American Institute of Indian Studies.

Krishnamachariar, M. 2004 (reprint. First ed. 1937). *History of Classical Sanskrit Literature*. Delhi: Motilal Banarsidass Publishers.

Krishnan, K. G. 2006. Distance Administration under Vijayanagara. In: *Recent Advances in Vijayanagara Studies*. Edited by P. Shanmugam and S. Srinivasan. Chennai: New Era Publications.

Kulke, H. 2001a. Functional Interpretation of a South Indian Māhātmya: The Legend of Hiraṇyavarman and the Life of the Cōḻa King Kulottuṅga. In: H. Kulke. *Kings and Cults. State Formation and Legitimation in India and Southeast Asia*. New Delhi: Manohar: 192–207.

—. 2001b. Mahārājas, Mahants and Historians: Reflections on the Historiography of Early Vijayanagara and Sringeri. In: H. Kulke. *Kings and Cults. State Formation and Legitimation in India and Southeast Asia*. New Delhi: Manohar: 208–239.

Kulke, H. and D. Rothermund. 1990. *A History of India*. 2nd ed. Routledge: London.

Lienhard, S. 1984. *History of Classical Poetry: Sanskrit, Pali, Prakrit*. Wiesbaden: Otto Harrassowitz.

Lingorska. M. 2007. Ich weiß nicht, liebe Freundin, warum mir das Herz nicht zerbricht: Dichterinnen in der klassischen indischen Literatur. In: V. Eschbach-Szabo & H. Buck-Albulet (ed). *Aktuelle Arbeiten und Vorträge an der Fakultät für Kulturwissenschaften der Universität Tübingen*. Eberhard Karls Universität Tübingen: 113–124.

Lorenzen, D. N. 1972. *The Kāpālikas and Kālāmukhas : two lost Śaivite sects*. Berkeley: University of California Press.

Mahalingam, T. V. 1967. *South Indian Polity*. University of Madras.

—. 1969 (2nd Edition). *Administration and Social Life under Vijayanagara. Part I. Administration*. Madras: Manorama Press.

—. 1975 (2nd Edition). *Administration and Social Life under Vijayanagara. Part II. Social Life*. Madras: Manorama Press.

Mallappa, T. N. 1974. *Kriyasakti Vidyaranya*. Bangalore: Bangalore University.

Mallebrein, C. and H. von Stietencron. 2008. *The Divine Play on Earth. Religious Aesthetics and Ritual in Orissa.* Heidelberg: Synchron Publishers.

Michell, G. 1995. *The New Cambridge History of India*, I, 6. *Architecture and Art of Southern India: Vijayanagara and the successor states.* Cambridge: Cambridge University Press.

Misra, S. 2007. *Rājarānī Gaṅgadevī aur unkā kāvyaśilp.* Delhi: Nag Publishers.

Monier–Williams, M. 2005 (reprint. First ed. 1899). *A Sanskrit–English Dictionary.* Delhi: Motilal Banarsidass.

Naraindas, H. 2009. A Sacramental Theory of Childbirth in India. In: H. Selin and P. K. Stone (eds.). *Childbirth across Cultures. Ideas and Practices of Pregnancy, Childbirth and the Postpartum.* Dordrecht–Heidelberg–London–New York: Springer: 95–106.

Nelson, J. H. 1989 (Reprint of 1868 ed.). *The political history of the Madura country : ancient and modern.* New Delhi: Asian Educational Services.

Palaniappan, K. 1970. *The Great Temple of Madurai. English Version of the Book "Koilmanagar".* Madurai: Sri Meenakshisundareswarar Temple Renovation Committee.

Pandey. R. 1969 (2nd Revised Edition). *Hindu Saṃskāras. Socio-religious Study of the Hindu Sacraments.* Delhi: Motilal Banarsidass Publishers.

Parasher-Sen, A. 2001. Renunciation in the Jain Tradition. In: S. Rajagopal (ed.). *Kaveri. Studies in Epigraphy, Archaeology and History (Professor Y. Subbarayalu Felicitation Volume).* Chennai: Panpattu Veliyiitakam.

Pigoniowa, M. 2005. The lament of Rati. In: L. Sudyka (ed.). *Cracow Indological Studies.* Vol. 7: 69–80.

Pollock, Sh. 1993. Rāmyāṇa and Political Imagination in India. *The Journal of Asian Studies*. Vol. 52, No 2: 261–297.

—. 1996. The Sanskrit Cosmopolis, 300–1300 CE: Transculturation, Vernacularization, and the Question of Ideology. In: J. E. M. Houben (ed.). *Ideology and status of Sanskrit : contributions to the history of the Sanskrit language*. Leiden–New York–Köln: E.J. Brill.

Prabha, C. 1976. *Historical Mahākāvyas in Sanskrit*. New Delhi: Shri Bharat Bharati.

Rajagopal, S. 2001. *Kaveri. Studies in Epigraphy, Archaeology and History (Professor Y. Subbarayalu Felicitation Volume)*. Chennai: Panpattu Veliyiitakam.

Rajendran, C. 2008. Business unusual: Bāṇa's description of Dawn in *Harṣacarita*. In: L. Sudyka (ed.). *Cracow Indological Studies*. Vol. 9: 141–146.

Ram, K. 2009. Rural Midwives in South India: The Politics of Bodily Knowledge. In: H. Selin and P. K. Stone (eds.). *Childbirth across Cultures. Ideas and Practices of Pregnancy, Childbirth and the Postpartum*. Dordrecht–Heidelberg–London–New York: Springer: 107–122.

Ramanujan, A. K. 2004. Towards an Anthology of City Images. In: V. Dharwadker. *The Collected esseys of A. K. Ramanujan*. New Delhi: Oxford University Press.

Ramanujan, A. K., V. N. Rao and D. Shulman (eds. & transl.). 1994. *When God is a Customer. Telugu Courtesan Songs by Kṣetrayya and Others*. Berkeley–Los Angeles–London: University of California Press.

Rangacharya, M. and S. Kuppuswami Sastri. 1918. *A Triennial Catalogue of Manuscripts 1910–11 to 1912–13 for the Governmental Oriental Manuscript Library Madras*. Vol. IV, Part. I, Part III. Madras: Government Press.

Rangasvami Sarasvati, A. 1925. Political Maxims of the Emperor Poet, Krishna Devaraya. *Journal of Indian History* 6.

Rao, V. N. 1995. Coconut and Honey: Sanskrit and Telugu in Medieval Andhra. *Social Scientist*. Vol. 23, nos. 10–12: 24–40.

Rao, V. N. and D. Shulman (coll. and transl.) 1998. *A poem at the right moment : remembered verses from premodern South India*. Berkeley–Los Angeles–London: University of California Press.

Rao, V. N., D. Shulman and S. Subrahmanyam. 1998. *Symbols of Substance, Court and State in Nāyaka Period Tamilnadu*. Delhi: Oxford University Press.

—. 2006 (First Ed. 2001). *Textures of Time: Writing History in South India 1600–1800*. Delhi: Permanent Black.

Redfield, R. and M. B. Singer. 1954. The Cultural Role of Cities. *Economic Development and Cultural Change* 3 (1): 53-73.

Rice, B. L. 1909. *Mysore and Coorg from the Inscriptions*. London: Archibald Constable & Co. Ltd.

Rocher, L. 1986. *The Purāṇas*. Wiesbaden: Harrasowitz.

Saletore, A. B. 1933. *Social and Political Life in the Vijayanagara Empire (A.D. 1346–A.D. 1646)*. Vol. 1–2. Madras: B.G. Paul & Co. Publishers.

—. 1992 (reprint. First published 1936). Theories Concerning the Origin of Vijayanagara. *Vijayanagara Sexcentenary Commemoration Volume*. Dharwar: Vijayanagara Empire Sexcentenary Association, 139–159.

Sarma, S. R. 1979. *Saluva Dynasty of Vijayanagar*. Hyderabad: Prabhakar Publications.

Sarup, L. 1933. A queen poetess of Vijayanagara. In: O. Stein and W. Gampert (eds.). *Festschrift Moriz Winternitz*. Leipzig: Otto Harrassowitz: 92–97.

Sastri, Kuppuswami S. 1917. *A Triennial Catalogue of Manuscripts.* Vol. II, Part I. Madras: Government Press.

Sastri Nilakanta, K. A. 1964. *Sources of Indian History with special references to South India.* Bombay–Calcutta–New Delhi–Madras–Lucknow–London–New York: Asia Publishing House.

—. 1955. *A History of South India from Prehistoric Times to the Fall of Vijayanagar.* Madras: Oxford University Press.

Sethuraman, N. 1987. The Sambuvarayas of the 14th Century. In: *Journal of the Epigraphical Society of India* 13: 12–29

Settar, S. 1989. *Inviting Death: Indian attitude towards the ritual death.* Leiden: E.J. Brill.

Settar, S. and G. D. Sontheimer (eds.). 1982. *Memorial Stones: A Study of Their Origin, Significance, and Variety.* Dharwad: Institute of Indian Art History, Karnatak University.

Sewell, R. 1992 (reprint). *A Forgotten Empire (Vijayanagar). A Contribution to the History of India.* New Delhi–Madras: Asian Educational Service.

Sharma, S. 2005. *Amir Khusraw: The Poet of Sufis and Sultans.* Oxford: Oneworld.

Sinopoli, C. M. 2004. Beyond Vijayanagara's City Walls: Regional Survey and the Inhabitants of the Vijayanagar Metropolitan Region. In: H. P. Ray and C. M. Sinopoli (eds.). *Archaeology as History in Early South Asia.* New Delhi: Indian Council of Historical Research.

Singer, M. 1966. The Rādhā-Krishna Bhajanas of Madras City. In: M. Singer (ed.). *Krishna: Myths, Rites, and Attitudes.* Chicago–London: The University of Chicago Press: 90–138.

Smith, D. 1985. *Ratnākara's Haravijaya. An Introduction to the Sanskrit Court Epic.* Delhi: Oxford University Press.

—. 2000. An Alternative Poetics of the Lotus. In: J. Vacek (ed.). *Pandanus 2000: Natural Symbolism in Indian Literatures.* Prague: Signeta: 211–230.

—. 2005. Kissing in *kāvya*, with special reference to Kālidāsa's *Kumārasaṃbhava.* In: L.Sudyka (ed.). *Cracow Indological Studies.* Vol. 7: 53-–68.

—. 2006. Animality and related realms of being in Bāṇa's *Kādambarī'.* In: J. Vacek (ed.). *Pandanus* 06. Prague: Signeta: 79–92.

—. 2012. One man and many women: some notes on the harem in mainly ancient and medieval India from sundry perspectives. In: L.Sudyka (ed.). *Cracow Indological Studies.* Vol. 14: 1–16.

Sontheimer, G.-D. 1985. Folk Deities in the Vijayanagara Empire: Narasimha and Mallanna. In: A. L. Dallapiccola and S. Zingel-Lallemant (eds.). *The Kingdom of Vijayanagara.* Int. Vijayanagara Seminar in Heidelberg, July I983. Wiesbaden: 144–158.

—. 1997. *King of Hunters, Warriors and Shepherds: Essays on Khaṇḍobā.* Ed. by Anne Feldhaus, Aditya Malik, Heidrun Brückner. New Delhi: Indira Gandhi National Centre for the Arts: Manohar.

Stein, B. 1980. *Peasant State and Society in Medieval South India.* Delhi: Oxford University Press.

—. 1997 (reprint of 1993 ed.). *Vijayanagara.* The New Cambridge History of India. I.2. Delhi: Cambridge University Press.

Steiner, M. 2010. Truth Under the Guise of Poetry: Aśvaghoṣa's "Life of the Buddha". In: L. Covill, U. Roesler and S. Shaw (eds.). *Lives Lived, Lives Imagined. Biography in the Buddhist Traditions.* Boston: Wisdom Publications, The Oxford Centre for Buddhist Studies: 89–122.

Sudyka, L. 2003. From Aśvaghoṣa to Bhaṭṭi: the development of the *mahākāvya* genre. In: H. Marlewicz and R. Czekalska (eds.). *Cracow Indological Studies*. Vol. 4/5: 509–528.

—. 2004a. Flowers and Love in Sanskrit Kāvya Poetry. The Arrows of Kāmadeva. In: O. Botto, G. Boccali and P. M. Rossi (eds.). *Atti del Seminario "La Natura nel Pensiero, nella Letteratura e nelle Arti dell'India"*. Associazione Italiana di Studi Sanscriti. Torino: 121–145.

—. 2004b. *Od Ramajany do dydaktyki, czyli zagadki 'Poematu Bhattiego'*. Kraków: Księgarnia Akademicka.

—. 2009. Cennapurī—a City of Gardens as Described in the *Sarvadevavilāsa* and theRemnants of the Gardens and Garden Houses Today. *Pandanus 09*. Vol. 3/1: 22–35; 105–134.

—. 2010. Vijayanagara City as Described in the *Madhurāvijaya* and *Acyutarāyābhudaya*. In: D. Stasik and A. Trynkowska (eds.). *The City and the Forest in Indian Literature and Arts*. Warsaw: Dom Wydawniczy Elipsa: 98–113.

—. 2011. *Kirātārjunīya* in South India: the story as depicted in literature and art with a special reference to the Lepakshi temple. In: L. Sudyka (ed.). *Interrelations of Indian Literature and Art*. Kraków: Księgarnia Akademicka: 145–162.

—. (forthcoming). War expedition or pilgrimage? Acyutarāya's southern campaign as depicted in the *Acyutarāyābhyudaya*.

Sulocana Devi, L. 1992. *A Historical Survey of Sanskrit Mahākāvyas*. Delhi: Kanishka Publishing House.

Szczepanik, L. 2010. *How to Teach Sanskrit Grammar. The Case of the Perfect System in the Bhaṭṭikāvya*. Unpublished M.A. dissertation. Jagiellonian University, Kraków.

Świdzińska, N. 2003. Some remarks on memorial stones tradition in Tamil Nadu. In: R. Czekalska and H. Marlewicz (eds.). *Cracow Indological Studies*. Vol. 4–5: 577–586.

—. 2007. The Cult of the Dead and Memorial Stones in Classical Tamil Literature, Stone Inscriptions and Iconography. In: D. Stasik and A. Trynkowska. *Teaching on India in Central and Eastern Europe*. Warsaw: Dom Wydawniczy Elipsa: 161–170.

Talbot, C. 1995 Inscribing the Other, Inscribing the Self: Hindu-Muslim Identities in Pre-Colonial India. In: *Comparative Studies in Society and History*. Vol. 37, No. 4 (Oct., 1995). Cambridge University Press: 692-722.

—. 2001. *Precolonial India in Practice. Society, Region, and Identity in Medieval Andhra*. Oxford–New York: Oxford University Press.

Trynkowska, A. 2000. Mallinātha and Classical Indian Theoreticians of Literature on Descriptions in the *Mahākāvya*. In: L. Sudyka (ed.). *Cracow Indological Studies*. Vol. 2: 37–48.

—. (forthcoming). Political metaphors in the *mahākāvya*: The conceptual metaphor the state is the human body in Māgha's *Śiśupālavadha*. In: L. Sudyka and A. Nitecka (eds.). *Cracow Indological Studies*. Vol. 15.

Tubb, G. 1984. Heroine as Hero: Parvati in the Kumarasambhava and the Parvatiparinaya. In: *Journal of the American Oriental Society*. Vol. 104, No. 2, April-June, 1984: 219–236.

Vassilkov, Y. 2011. Indian "hero-stones" and the Earliest Anthropomorphic Stelae of the Bronze Age. In: *Journal of Indo-European Studies*. Vol. 39, No. 1 & 2, Spring/Summer 2011.

—. (forthcoming a). The Mahābhārata and Non-Vedic Aryan Traditions In: M. Ježić (ed.). *Proceedings of the Fifth Dubrovnik International Conference on the Sanskrit Epics and Purāṇas*. Zagreb: Croatian Academy of Science.

—. (forthcoming b). Animal symbolism of warrior brotherhoods in Indian epic, culture and history. In: T. Pontillo (ed.)

Vrātyas and Surrounds. The broken world of sovereignty in India and beyond.

Venkataramanayya, N. 1933. *Vijayanagara: origin of the city and the empire.* Madras: Madras University.

Venkateswaran, T. K. 1966. Rādhā-Krishna *Bhajanas* of South India. A Phenomenological, Theological, and Philosophical Study. In: Milton Singer (ed.). *Krishna: Myths, Rites, and Attitudes.* Chicago–London: The University of Chicago Press: 139–172.

Vogel, J.P. 1962. *The Goose in Indian Literature and Art.* Leiden: E. J. Brill.

Wagoner, Ph. B. 1993. *Tidings of the King. A translation and Ethnohistorical Analysis of the Rāyavācakamu.* Honolulu: University of Hawaii Press.

—. 1996a. From"Pampa's Crossing" to the "Place of Lord Virupaksha": Architecture, Cult, and Patronage at Hampi Before the Founding of Vijayanagara. In: D. Devaraj and C. S. Pahl (eds.). *Vijayanagara: Progress of Research 1988–91.* Directorate of Archaeology and Museums. Mysore: 141–174.

—. 1996b. Sultan among Hindu Kings: Dress, Titles, and the Islamicisation of Hindu Culture at Vijayanagara. *Journal of Asian Studies* 55. No. 4 (Nov. 1996): 851–880.

—. 2000. Harihara, Bukka, and the Sultan: The Delhi Sultanate in the Political Imagination of Vijayanagara. In: D. Gilmartin and B. B. Lawrence (eds.). *Beyond Turk and Hindu.* Gainesville: University Press of Florida: 312–315.

Wiswanathan Peterson, I. 2003. *Design and Rhetoric in a Sanskrit Court Epic:The Kirātārjunīya of Bhāravi.* Albany: State University of New York Press.

Index